CULTURE ART EDUCATION EXCHANGE RESOURCE

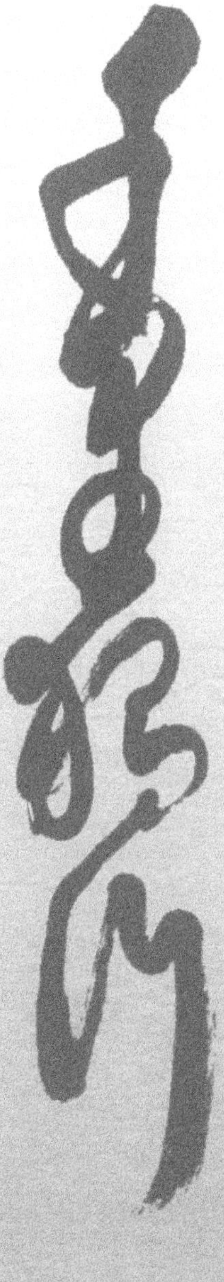

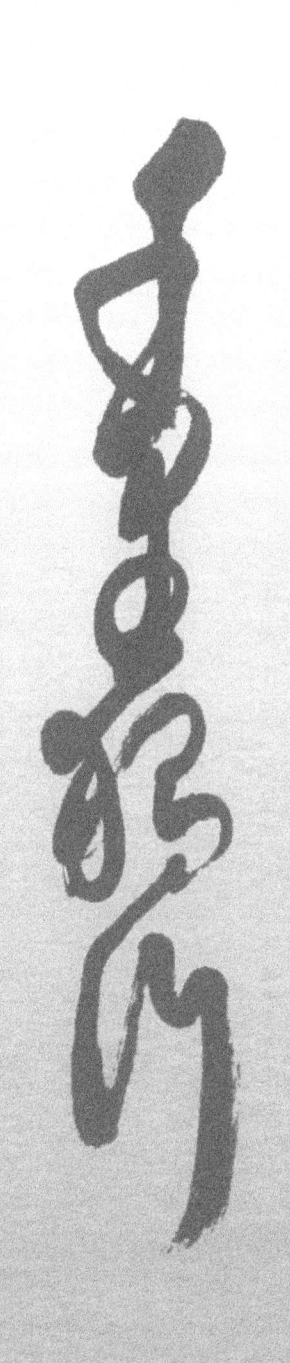

THIÊN LÝ ĐỘC HÀNH
Thơ Tuệ Sỹ

Dịch sang tiếng Hán-Nôm và tiếng Nhật 漢喃・和訳 | Bùi Chí Trung
Hán-Nôm and Japanese translation
Traduction en Hán-Nôm et Japonais

Dịch sang tiếng Anh 英訳 | Nguyễn Phước Nguyên
English translation
Traduction en Anglais

Dịch sang tiếng Pháp 仏訳 | Dominique de Miscault
French translation
Traduction en Français

UNE ODYSSEE INTERIEURE

Droit d'auteur @ 2023   Deuxième édition @ 2023
Tous les droits sont reserves. Aucune partie de ce livre ne peut être reproduite

CULTURE ART EDUCATION EXCHANGE RESOURCE
Bản quyền @ 2023 - Xuất bản lần thứ hai, 2023

ODYSSEY UNTO SELF
The Poetry of Tue Sy 詩

千里独行

Thủ bút Hán Nôm	漢喃筆	Tuệ Sỹ
Hán-Nôm hand writing		
Écriture manuelle Hán-Nôm		

Hình ảnh 写真 Hạnh Viên
Photography
Photos

Tranh phụ bản 絵
Painting illustration
Peintures illustrées — Đào Nguyên Dạ Thảo

Biên tập, Thiết kế bìa và Trình bày 編集・デザイン
Edit, Cover design and Layout
Rédaction et Design

本書の全部または一部を無断複写複製等は著作権法上で禁じられています。
Copyright @ 2023. All rights reserved. No part of this book may be reproduced

CULTURE ART EDUCATION EXCHANGE RESOURCE

2023 第 2 刷発行
Second Edition, 2023

Tuệ Sỹ sinh năm 1945 ở Paksé, Lào.

- 1954, xuất gia học pháp dòng Lâm Tế tại chùa Trang Nghiêm, làng Tân An, Paksé, Lào.
- 1960, về Việt Nam một mình, tự lập và sống nương nhờ các chùa tại Huế, Nha Trang, Sài Gòn, Tiền Giang và các tỉnh miền Nam.
- 1961, thọ Sa-di giới; sau về ở thiền viện Quảng Hương Già Lam, Sài Gòn.
- 1964, tốt nghiệp Viện Cao Đẳng Phật Học Sài Gòn.
- 1965, học tại Viện Đại Học Vạn Hạnh, Phân khoa Phật học.
- Từ 1966, viết văn làm thơ đăng báo và phụ trách biên tập một vài tạp chí văn triết học thời đó.
- Từ 1970, Giáo sư dạy Triết học Phật giáo, kiêm Tổng thư ký tòa soạn Tạp chí Tư Tưởng của Đại Học Vạn Hạnh.
- 1973, về Nha Trang làm Giám học Viện Cao Đẳng Phật Học Hải Đức.
- Sau biến cố 30/4/1975, về ở ẩn tại miếng rẫy chùa ở ven rừng Vạn Giã, cách Nha Trang 60 km.
- 1977, trở lại Sài Gòn lánh nạn.
- 1978 - 1980, bị nhà cầm quyền bắt giam 3 năm không xét xử (tội cư trú bất hợp pháp).
- 1981 - 1984, làm Giáo thọ sư cho khóa đào tạo đặc biệt tại thiền viện Quảng Hương Già Lam.
- Tháng 4/1984, bị bắt lại lần thứ hai cùng giáo sư Trí Siêu Lê Mạnh Thát.
- Tháng 9/1988, cả hai thầy đều bị tuyên án tử hình, một tháng sau giảm án xuống còn 20 năm khổ sai, trải qua các nhà tù ở Đồng Nai - miền Nam, Phú Yên - miền Trung và Ba Sao - miền Bắc.
- 03/8/1998, được Tổ chức Human Rights Watch trao giải thưởng tranh đấu nhân quyền Hellman/Hammett Award.
- 02/9/1998, được trả tự do và chính quyền đưa lên xe lửa, buộc phải về Nam.
- Từ 1998, dành nhiều thì giờ phiên dịch kinh điển và sáng tác; sống ở một am nhỏ trong rừng vùng Bảo Lộc.
- 03/12/2021, thành lập, Chủ tịch Hội đồng Phiên dịch Lâm thời Đại tạng Kinh Việt Nam.
- 21/8/2022, đảm nhiệm trách vụ Chánh Thư ký kiêm Xử lý Thường vụ Viện Tăng Thống GHPGVNTN.
- 24/11/2023, viên tịch tại Chùa Phật Ân, Đồng Nai ở tuổi 79.

觉悟众生

Tuệ Sỹ was born in 1945 in Paksé, Laos.

- 1954, he joined the Lâm Tế (Rinzai) School as a novice at Trang Nghiêm Pagoda in Tân An Village, Paksé, Laos.
- 1960, came back to Vietnam alone, was self-sufficient and sojourned throughout South Vietnam at many provincial temples in Huế, Nha Trang, Sài Gòn, Tiền Giang.
- 1961, he was ordained as a novice monk and later was accepted into the Quảng Hương Già Lam Zen Monastery in Sài Gòn.
- 1964, graduated from the Sài Gòn College of Buddhist Studies.
- 1965, studied at the Faculty of Buddhist Studies of Vạn Hạnh University, Sài Gòn.
- From 1966, his essays and poems were first published in literary magazines, for some of which he subsequently assumed editorship.
- 1970, he was appointed as a Professor of Buddhist Philosophy and Editor-in-chief of the University's magazine 'Tư Tưởng' (Thought) at Vạn Hạnh University.
- 1973, moved to Nha Trang, appointed as the Director of the Hải Đức College of Buddhist Studies.
- After the event of the April 30, 1975, he retreated to a monastery plot on the fringes of Vạn Giã forest, approximately 60 km from Nha Trang.
- 1977, relocated to Sài Gòn.
- 1978 - 1980, he was imprisoned for 3 years without trial (offense of inhabiting without notice to the authorities).
- 1981 - 1984, was a Dharma Instructor for the Special Training Course at Quảng Hương Già Lam Zen Monastery.
- April 1984, he was detained again along with Professor Trí Siêu Lê Mạnh Thát.
- September 1988, both were sentenced to death. One month later, his death sentence was commuted to 20 years of hard labor, and imprisoning first at Đồng Nai - South Vietnam, then at Phú Yên - Midland and finally at Ba Sao - North Vietnam.
- August 03, 1998, he was presented the Hellman/Hammett Award from the Human Rights Watch.
- September 02, 1998, he was released and deported back to the South by train.
- From 1998, he devoted most of his time to writing and translating scriptures in a remote hermitage in the plateau of Bảo Lộc.
- December 03, 2021, he established and was designated President of the Provisional Tripitaka Translation Council.
- August 21, 2022, he was chosen to assume the responsibilities of the Chief Secretary cum Standing Chief Executor of the Supreme Central Council of Unified Buddhist Church of Vietnam.
- November 24, 2023, he serenely passed away at Phật Ân Temple, Đồng Nai at the age of 79.

ODYSSEY UNTO SELF

Tuệ Sỹ est né en 1945 à Paksé, au Laos.

- 1954, ordonné Lâm Tế (Rinzai) Dharma à la pagode Trang Nghiêm, Tân An village, Paksé, Laos.
- 1960, retourne au Vietnam seul et indépendant, et séjourne dans de nombreux temples provinciaux du Vietnam du Sud: Huế, Nha Trang, Sài Gòn et Tiền Giang.
- 1961, ordonné moine novice, et après il est entré au monastère Zen de Quảng Hương Già Lam à Sài Gòn.
- 1964, diplômé du Collège Bouddhiste de Sài Gòn.
- 1965, études à la Faculté d'Études Bouddhistes de l'Université Vạn Hạnh, Sài Gòn.
- Depuis 1966, il écrit des poèmes et des courts romans, publie des articles et édite quelques ouvrages philosophiques.
- Depuis 1970, il enseigne la philosophie bouddhiste et devient rédacteur en chef du magazine Tư Tưởng (Pensée) à l'Université Vạn Hạnh.
- 1973, retourne à Nha Trang, nommé coordinateur académique du Collège Bouddhiste de Hải Đức.
- Après les évènements du 30 avril 1975, retiré dans une parcelle de monastère en bordure de la forêt de Vạn Giã, à environ 60 km de Nha Trang.
- 1977, déménagement à Saigon.
- 1978-1980, il est arrêté et emprisonné pendant trois ans sans jugement (infraction: résidence sans préavis à l'autorité).
- 1981-1984, il était instructeur Maître du Dharma au Cours de formation spéciale au monastère Zen de Quảng Hương Già Lam.
- Avril 1984, il est arrêté à nouveau avec le professeur Trí Siêu Lê Mạnh Thát.
- Septembre 1988, les deux furent condamnés à mort. Un mois plus tard, sa peine est commuée en 20 ans de travaux forcés; et l'emprisonnement d'abord à Đồng Nai - Sud, puis à Phú Yên - région centrale, et enfin à Ba Sao - Nord du pays.
- 03 Août 1998, il reçoit le prix Hellman/Hammett de Human Rights Watch.
- 02 Septembre 1998, il est libéré et forcé de retourner au Sud par le train.
- Depuis 1998, passe beaucoup de temps à traduire des Écritures et à composer; il vit dans un petit hermitage sur le plateau de Bảo Lộc.
- 03 Decembre 2021, il a établi et a été désigné président du Conseil provisoire de traduction de Tripitaka.
- 21 Août 2022, il est choisi pour Secrétaire général en charge des relations internes de l'Eglise bouddhiste unifiée du Vietnam.
- 24 Novembre 2023, il décède sereinement à l'âge de 79 ans au temple Phật Ân, à Đồng Nai.

Une Odyssée Intérieure

Senridokkoo

Tuệ Sỹ (慧士) は1945年ラオスのPakséに生まれた。

- 1954、ラオス・PakséのTân An村において臨済宗Trang Nghiêm寺に出家。
- 1960、ベトナムに単身帰国・自立し、Huế、Nha Trang、Sài Gòn、Tiền Giang及び南部各省の諸寺に転々して生活。
- 1961、受戒。その後Sài GònのQuảng Hương Già Lam禅院に入る。
- 1964、Sài Gòn仏教高等学院を卒業。
- 1965、Sài GònのVạn Hạnh大学仏教学科在学。
- 1966より、詩や小説を執筆しながら、その時代の文学哲学雑誌等の編集委員を務める。
- 1970より、Vạn Hạnh大学の仏教哲学担当教授及び大学雑誌Tư Tưởng（思想）編集長を務める。
- 1973、Nha Trangに戻り、Hải Đức仏教高等学院の監学職を務める。
- 1975/4/30政変後、Nha Trangより60 km離れるVạn Giãの森に寺の畑を耕し隠居生活。
- 1977、避難のためSài Gònに戻る。
- 1978-1980、居住無届けの理由で逮捕、無裁判で3年間投獄された。
- 1981-1984、Quảng Hương Già Lam禅院にて特別研修会の教授師を務める。
- 1984/4、Trí Siêu Lê Mạnh Thát教授と共に再逮捕された。
- 1988/9、二人とも死刑宣告されたが翌月に20年労役に減刑、Đồng Nai-南部、Phú Yên-中部、Ba Sao-北部の各刑務所に収容されていた。
- 1998/8/03、ヒューマン・ライツ・ウォッチよりヘルマン・ハメット賞を受賞。
- 1998/9/02、釈放され、強制的に列車で南部へ戻される。
- 1998よりベトナム・Bảo Lộcの森に小庵を建て経典翻訳や著述中心の生活を送る。
- 2021/12/03、臨時大蔵経翻訳委員会設立、委員長を務める。
- 2022/8/21、ベトナム統一仏教教会僧統院常務執行委員及び事務総長を務める。
- 2023/11/24、Đồng Nai省Phật Ân寺にて示寂、79歳。

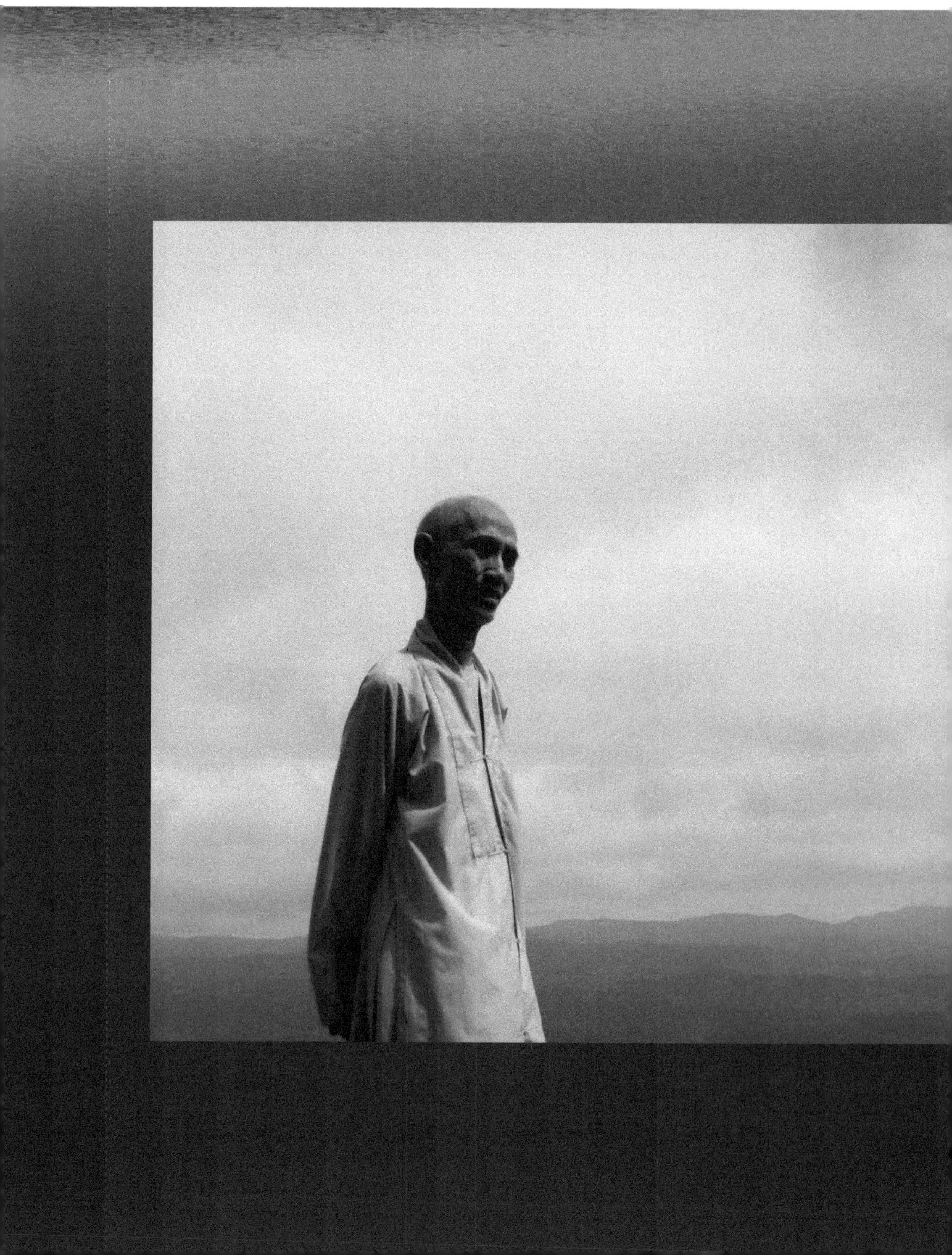

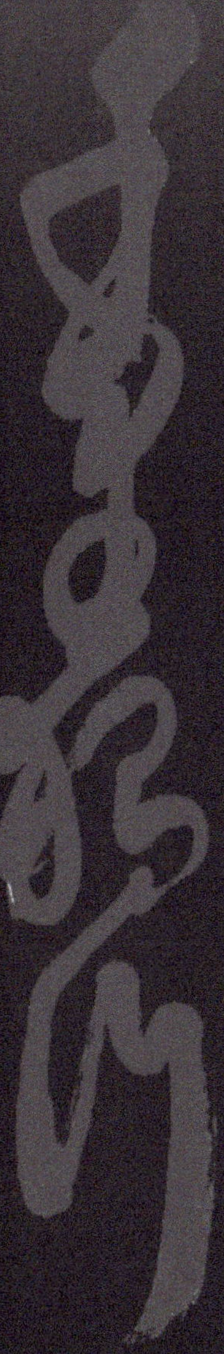

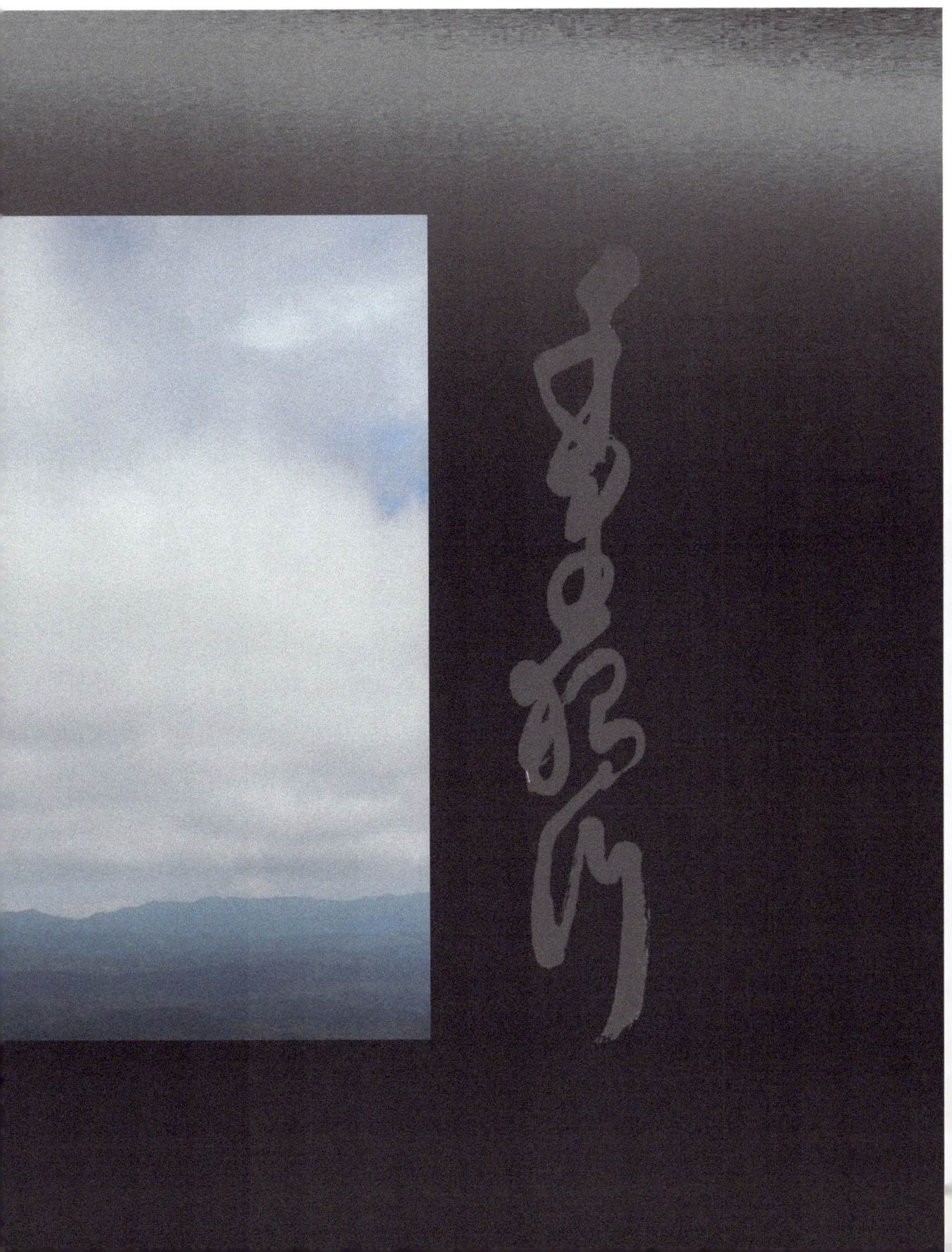

I.

Thơ Tuệ Sỹ

THIÊN LÝ ĐỘC HÀNH

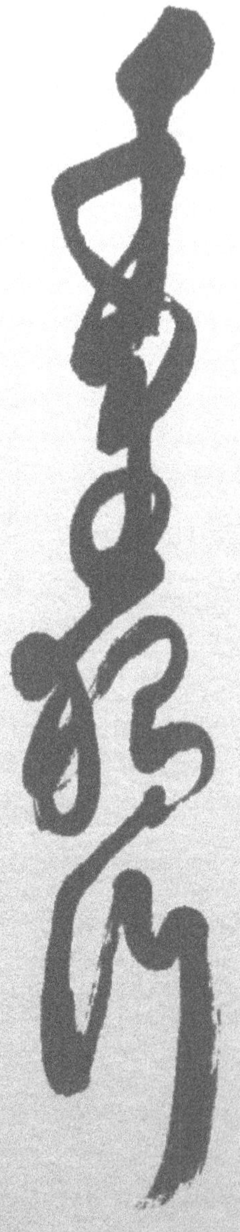

THIÊN LÝ ĐỘC HÀNH

Thơ Tuệ Sỹ

學佛沒燈心如
物般過去波中還矣
星懷沒了禪都差
奴中愛悞絕岸姊露

学佛

THIÊN LÝ ĐỘC HÀNH

1

Ta về một cõi tâm không
Vẫn nghe quá khứ ngập trong nắng tàn
Còn yêu một thuở đi hoang
Thu trong đáy mắt sao ngàn nửa khuya

藝術

些 術 沒 埃 心 空
吻 瞶 過 去 汲 氃 曩 殘
群 愯 沒 睥 㲚 荒
收 氃 坻 眛 猩 岸 牧 昂

少鼓

鳥低花尚啼

岭鼓

些	迻	蹶	曩	扁	嶂	
眊	疠	魂	骷	攄	遶	晙	暚
原	初	羅	儀	幺	翹	
嚾	叨	倒	論	寂	廖	浚	坡
群	低	船	岗	豬	爲	
酐	醉	些	買	蹲	踪	頂	高

THIÊN LÝ ĐỘC HÀNH

2

Ta đi dẫm nắng bên đèo
Nghe đau hồn cỏ rủ theo bóng chiều
Nguyên sơ là dáng yêu kiều
Bỗng đâu đảo lộn tịch liêu bến bờ
Còn đây góc núi trơ vơ
Nghìn năm ta mãi đứng chờ đỉnh cao

安
み
山京

密嶺
嘗持新茶歸膝視兒

蜜嫁

扁 嵊 屈 廟 孤 魂
羧 歪 幻 影 執 爐 華 燈
核 褥 晫 曝 爬 瀾
些 掩 鈷 呆 傔 怔 瞻 包

THIỀN LÝ ĐỘC HÀNH

3

Bên đèo khuất miễu cô hồn
Lưng trời ảo ảnh chập chờn hoa đăng
Cây già bóng tối bò lan
Ta ôm cỏ dại mơ màng chiêm bao

打雨

免余
罢些謎私烟絕裳

打盹

牞　某　舒　醉　待　瘊　疴
晬　得　孤　独　跌　黄　昏
罷　些　魂　硶　呸　牟　曡
掩　錀　坡　葟　覸　絪　慍

THIÊN LÝ ĐỘC HÀNH

4

Đã mấy nghìn năm đợi mỏi mòn
Bóng người cô độc dẫm hoàng hôn
Bởi ta hồn đá phơi màu nắng
Ôm trọn bờ lau kín nỗi buồn

自误

自	腂	洪	荒	些	於	叨
觎	些	核	蘿	包	舐	牟
眣	瞕	敲	釗	曾	唏	咀
溼	曠	魂	埃	馳	檩	莘

THIÊN LÝ ĐỘC HÀNH

5

Từ thuở hồng hoang ta ở đâu
Quanh ta cây lá đã thay màu
Chợt nghe xao xuyến từng hơi thở
Thấp thoáng hồn ai trong khóm lau

祖拱涪空
兀無霤浚
叭淨塘車
高屹襖身
嵊青岐前
頂霜些凳
車棲自想

蓮頂

THIÊN LÝ ĐỘC HÀNH

6

Trên đỉnh đèo cao bát ngát trông
Rừng mây xanh ngắt tạnh vô cùng
Từ ta trải áo đường mưa bụi
Tưởng thấy tiền thân trên bến không

崎南

欺 術 我 籤 嘲 僥
扁 嶸 群 覘 褸 荸 待 跦
沈 淪 自 眤 班 初
身 魸 些 吻 巴 爲 涪 塘

THIÊN LÝ ĐỘC HÀNH

7

Khi về ngả nón chào nhau
Bên đèo còn hẹn rừng lau đợi chờ
Trầm luân từ buổi ban sơ
Thân sau ta vẫn bơ vơ bụi đường

临摹

菩提門

晨岸

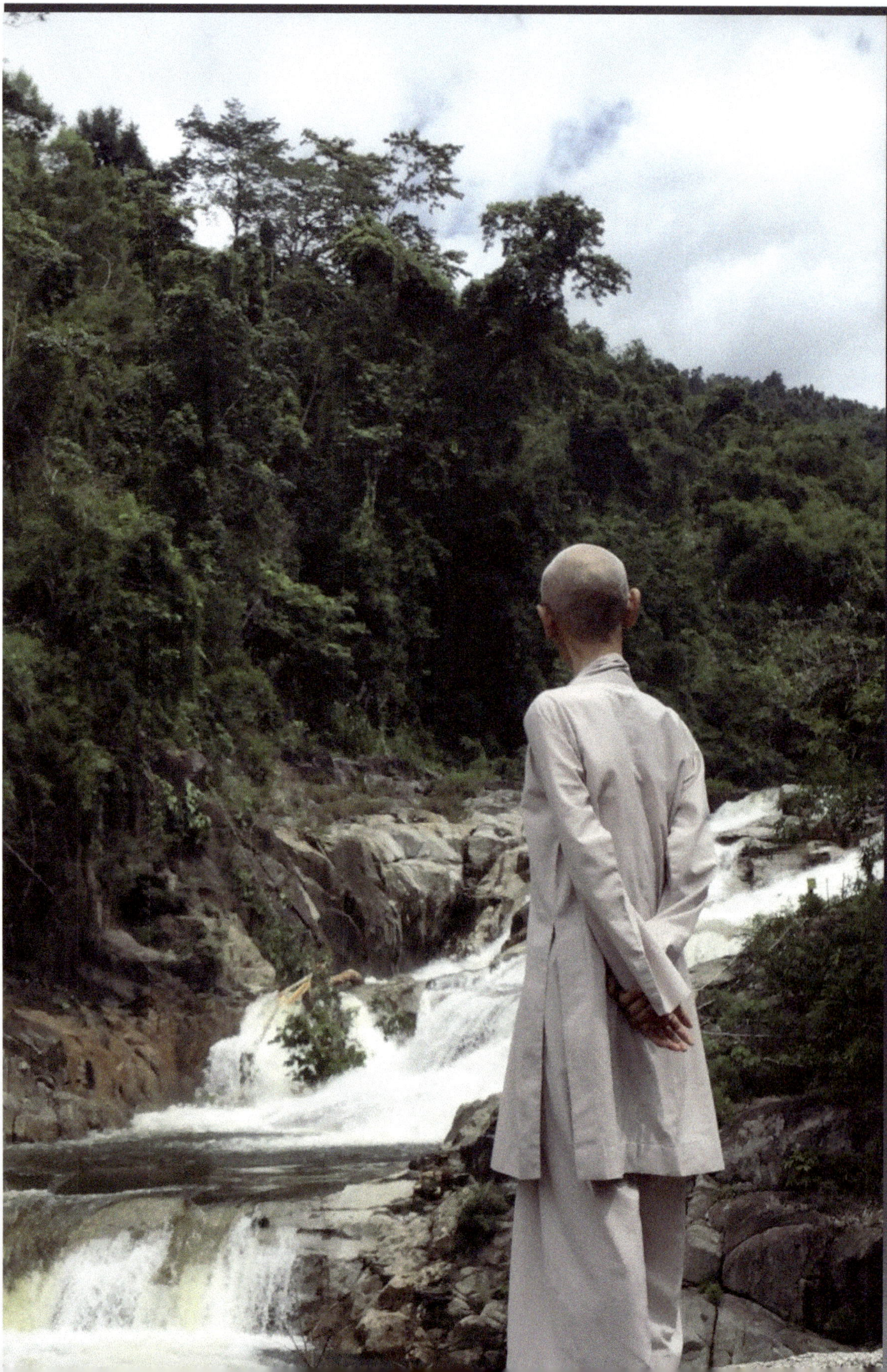

THIÊN LÝ ĐỘC HÀNH

8

Bóng tối sập mưa rừng tuôn thác đổ
Đường chênh vênh vách đá dọa nghiêng trời
Ta lầm lũi bóng ma tròn thế kỷ
Rủ nhau đi cùng tận cõi luân hồi
Khắp phố thị ngày xưa ta ruổi ngựa
Ngang qua đây ma quỷ khóc thành bầy
Lên hay xuống mắt mù theo nước lũ
Dẫm bàn chân lăn cát sỏi cùng trôi
Rồi ngã xuống nghe suối tràn ngập máu
Thân là thân cỏ lá gập ghềnh xuôi
Chờ mưa tạnh ta trải trăng làm chiếu
Nghìn năm sau hoa trắng trổ trên đồi

揿事

揿	事	情	悝	莞	骷	椄
些	術	舖	市	罷	情	鍾
掉	茷	香	蕊	旺	魂	磙
深	潘	眦	淵	霜	某	層

THIÊN LÝ ĐỘC HÀNH

9

Gởi lại tình yêu ngọn cỏ rừng
Ta về phố thị bởi tình chung
Trao đời hương nhụy phơi hồn đá
Thăm thẳm mù khơi sương mấy tầng

沒有

礌	矽	身	時	沒
漯	遶	躋	沚	曩
吟	潘	搽	荤	共
辕	懲	包	得	噲

THIÊN LÝ ĐỘC HÀNH

10

Một thời thân đá cuội
Nắng chảy dọc theo suối
Cọng lau già trầm ngâm
Hỏi người bao nhiêu tuổi

講故

跐	拸	瞕	鞈	動
拸	買	成	心	空
婚	吸	棧	如	夢
執	繵	霜	塊	齟

THIÊN LÝ ĐỘC HÀNH

11

Bước đi nghe cỏ động
Đi mãi thành tâm không
Hun hút rừng như mộng
Chập chùng mây khói trông

午橋

身	接	遠	晤	接	晤
眈	毧	余	蘿	檂	穟
燴	遠	塭	黏	漩	矽
吵	吻	群	印	跖	类

THIÊN LÝ ĐỘC HÀNH

12

Thân tiếp theo thân ngày tiếp ngày
Mù trong dư ảnh lá rừng bay
Dõi theo lối cũ bên triền đá
Sao vẫn còn in dấu lạc loài

簫 乖 棋 汝 英 術 欺
得 埃 空 高 嵊 冷 霅

放佛

THIỀN LÝ ĐỘC HÀNH

13

Khi về anh nhớ cài quai nón
Mưa lạnh đèo cao không cõi người

NÓI GÓT

THIÊN LÝ ĐỘC HÀNH

Một buổi sáng cuối thu năm 2011, đang ngồi trong quán cà-phê sách ở Đà lạt tôi nhận được mẩu tin của thầy gởi qua email, chỉ ngắn gọn mấy dòng:
...
Tôi đi lang thang theo đám mây trôi, phương trời vô định. Bờ sông, hốc núi, đâu cũng là chỗ vùi thây. Một chút duyên còn ràng buộc thì còn có cơ hội ngộ, đời này hoặc đời sau.
Thị ngạn am vô trụ xứ.

Thư được gởi đi từ chiều hôm trước, nghĩa là tối đó ông đã lang thang đâu đó ngoài bến xe, tìm một chuyến xe nào bất cứ, đi đến một nơi nào khả dĩ, không hẹn trước. Chuyến đi của ông thầy tu không chùa, không đệ tử, không cần nơi đến. Ra đi như vậy, ngoài những ẩn tình riêng chung, nhưng kỳ cùng nó là một thôi thúc, một bó buộc đã sẵn có tự bao giờ. Và trở về, cũng là một thôi thúc, bó buộc khác.

Gởi lại tình yêu ngọn cỏ rừng
Ta về phố thị bởi tình chung
Trao đời hương nhụy phơi hồn đá
Thăm thẳm mù khơi sương mấy từng

Thiên lý độc hành, chuỗi thơ 13 bài, hình thành sau chuyến đi ấy. Nó mở đầu bằng sự trở về, và kết thúc bằng lời gởi gắm một bước chân khác lên đường. Đi cho hết con đường thăm thẳm nhân sinh trường mộng. Hai câu kết để ta đóng lại tập thơ mà không đóng lại được những tâm tình khắc khoải, tương điệu trước một vệt nắng chiều, hay một ánh sao xa lay lắt cuối trời. Lời nhắn nhủ cuối thơ không phải là sự êm đềm khép lại cánh cổng vườn nhà sau khi người con đã trở về, nó mở ra lối sau chỉ về một phương trời khác tịch liêu...

Mưa lạnh
    đèo cao
        không cõi người.

Phương trời mờ ảo với ánh sao đêm làm đèn soi lối, lấy ánh trăng trên cỏ làm chiếu mà nằm, để sáng ra tiếp tục cuộc đi mà không biết đêm nay sẽ ở đâu, có 'may mắn' tìm được một chỗ ngủ kín gió không. Có khi chỗ đó là cái miếu cô hồn bên đèo vắng, có khi là phía sau cái bệ con sư tử đá khổng lồ trước cổng tam quan một ngôi chùa, nơi có một hốc nhỏ đủ cho một người nằm khuất tầm nhìn khách qua đường. Nghỉ chân và chợp mắt, để ba giờ khuya thức dậy thu vén đi tiếp trước khi nhịp sống đô thị trở lại nơi này cho một ngày mới. *Thân tiếp theo thân ngày tiếp ngày. Mù trong dư ảnh lá rừng bay…*

Cái mùi hoang liêu dặm trường sao mà huyễn hoặc. Nó hấp dẫn như mùi trái cây chín dại ven đường, như mấy gói lạc rang của một thanh niên tốt bụng đưa cho, để chiều lên đèo, "vì ở đó trong tầm bán kính mười cây số không có nhà ai", anh ta nói. Mấy gói lạc rang, đủ cho một ngày đi qua cái đèo hoang vu này.

Sau này họa hoằng được nghe kể về chuyến đi, tôi thấy thật khó viết được gì chân xác về những bài thơ này. Đó là những con đường nắng chát bụi bặm, những bầu trời tối sầm trĩu nặng mây đen, những chiều bụng đói, những đêm hun hút ngó về một quê hương nào đã mất. Đó không phải là trang giấy trắng để ta cặm cụi ghi chú vài ý tưởng mộng mơ. Tập thơ này với tôi không phải để đọc, để hiểu hay để viết về; chỉ cần nhìn, cảm, và tưởng tượng. Tôi không lo khi đọc đôi chỗ không hiểu thơ nói gì, nhưng sẽ buồn nếu không tưởng tượng được khung trời nào trong những câu:

Từ ta trải áo đường mưa bụi
Tưởng thấy tiền thân trên bến không

Mưa, nắng, gió, bụi; những bước chân miệt mài đi qua rừng, qua phố, để làm gì, để tìm gì? Tìm gì trong màu hoàng hôn phơi trên hồn đá, cái bóng người xiêu đổ bên bờ lau sậy phất phơ nỗi buồn viễn xứ. Xứ sở nào của người, của đá, của những bông lau bay trắng bốn phương ngàn? Nắng, bụi, gió, mưa. *Thiên nhai hà xứ vô phương thảo*⁽*⁾. Cuối trời vạn nẻo nơi nào không có cỏ xanh. Một đứa bé chạy theo dúi vào tay ông ổ bánh ngọt, chỉ tay về ngôi nhà lụp xụp bên vệ đường: Má con biểu đưa cho ông. Cái tình người nó tự nhiên như cỏ non xanh tận chân trời. Cỏ xanh và hoa lau trắng, màu trắng hoang mang cả trời cô lữ. Giữa dòng ngựa xe phố thị hay trước thảo nguyên xanh ngút ngàn, ở đâu cũng có lúc bất chợt cảm thấy lạc loài, thấy tháng ngày hư ảo, ta muốn đi tìm một cái gì đó khác, đo đếm xem khoảng cách bao xa giữa hai bờ mộng thực. Có người đi trong chiều nắng quái, có kẻ đi trong những giấc mộng khẽ khàng. Nhưng ai cũng có thể nhìn đám bụi mờ dưới bước chân đi mà tự hỏi, không biết đó là tha hương, hay là cố quận?

Rồi ngã xuống nghe suối tràn ngập máu
Thân là thân cỏ lá gập ghềnh xuôi
Chờ mưa tạnh ta trải trăng làm chiếu
Nghìn năm sau hoa trắng trổ trên đồi.

Ánh trăng sau cơn mưa hiện ra lấp lánh trên cỏ,
như trải ra tấm chiếu hoa gấm ngọc ngà.

Nghìn năm sau... kể chuyện Thiên lý độc hành, có người ngay thẳng và thực tế sẽ hỏi: Đi như vậy, tự đọa đày như vậy để làm gì, ích lợi gì?

Những bước chân vô định kia có để lại chút dấu vết nào nơi đá cuội ven đường? Có lẽ không. Hoặc có để lại một giấc mơ bên hiên nhà tạm trú đêm qua; không biết mưa lũ cao nguyên rồi sẽ cuốn phăng nó về đâu? Mà Thiên lý độc hành là gì? Đâu phải chỉ là một chuyến đi. Cuộc đi không có khởi hành, không cần nơi đến, thì làm sao có sự kết thúc trở về.

⁽*⁾ 天涯何處無芳草, thơ Tô Đông Pha.

NÓI GÓT THIÊN LÝ ĐỘC HÀNH

Khi về anh nhớ cài quai nón
Mưa lạnh đèo cao không cõi người…

Hạnh Viên
Mùa hạ Canh tý, PL. 2564.

ODYSSEY UNTO SELF

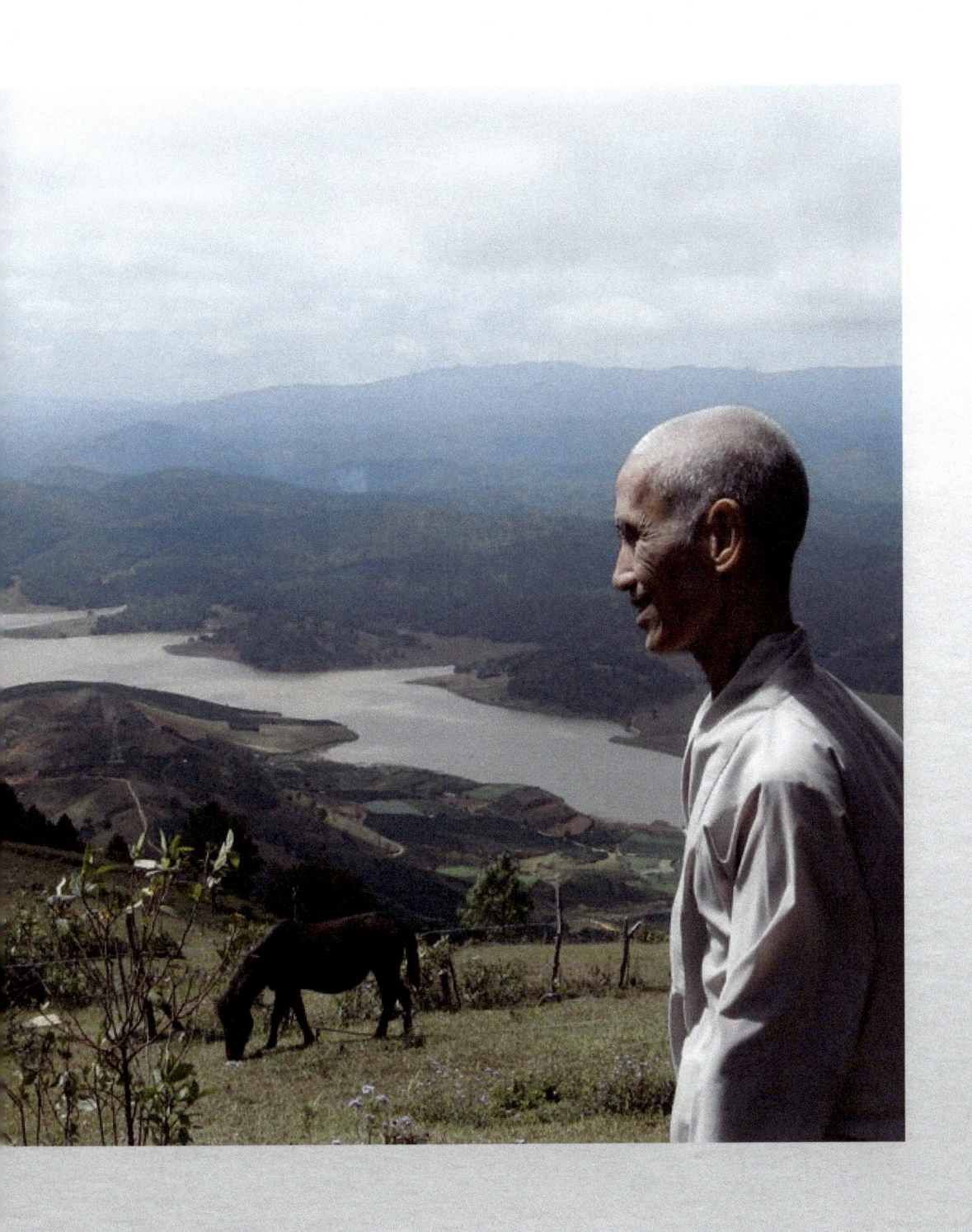

II. ODYSSEY UNTO SELF

Poetry of Tuệ Sỹ

ODYSSEY UNTO SELF

ODYSSEY UNTO SELF

ODYSSEY UNTO SELF

Poetry of Tuệ Sỹ

Odyssey Unto Self
1

Arrived empty-minded
My past inundated the fading sun
Still enamored with my wandering days
As nights of distance stars cocooned deep unto my eyes

Stepping on sunlight as I walked up a mountain pass
I felt the aching souls of grasses tilted into dusk
What was once gracefully primordial
Suddenly turned into shores of solitude
That ceded from a lonesome mountain corner
Whose peak I forever strived to reach

ODYSSEY UNTO SELF 2

O₃DYSSEY UNTO SELF

Hidden shrine for lost souls on a mountain pass
Mirages of lanterns flickered amidst the sky
Ancient tree shadows silently unfurled
As I dreamed tranquilly, cradling a blade of grass

Eons upon eons I wearily waited
A lonely shadow treading the eventide
For I was the soul of stone tinted by sunlight
Embracing ledges of reed to cover my sorrows

ODYSSEY UNTO SELF 4

ODYSSEY UNTO SELF
5

Whence came I since the dawn of creation
For leaves had altered colors around me
Suddenly I heard every breath quivered
As though a soul flittered among the reeds

ODYSSEY UNTO SELF 6

Immense, the view at the pass' peak
Forests, clouds, emerald vastness, quietude
Since my tunic spread onto roads of dusty rain
Upon the harbor of emptiness
I envisioned my past lived

ODYSSEY UNTO SELF
7

Bidding farewell with tilted hats
At mountain pass I pledged
My return to the waiting reed forest
Transmigrating tumultuously since time primordial
My afterlife would still be lonesome on its journeys

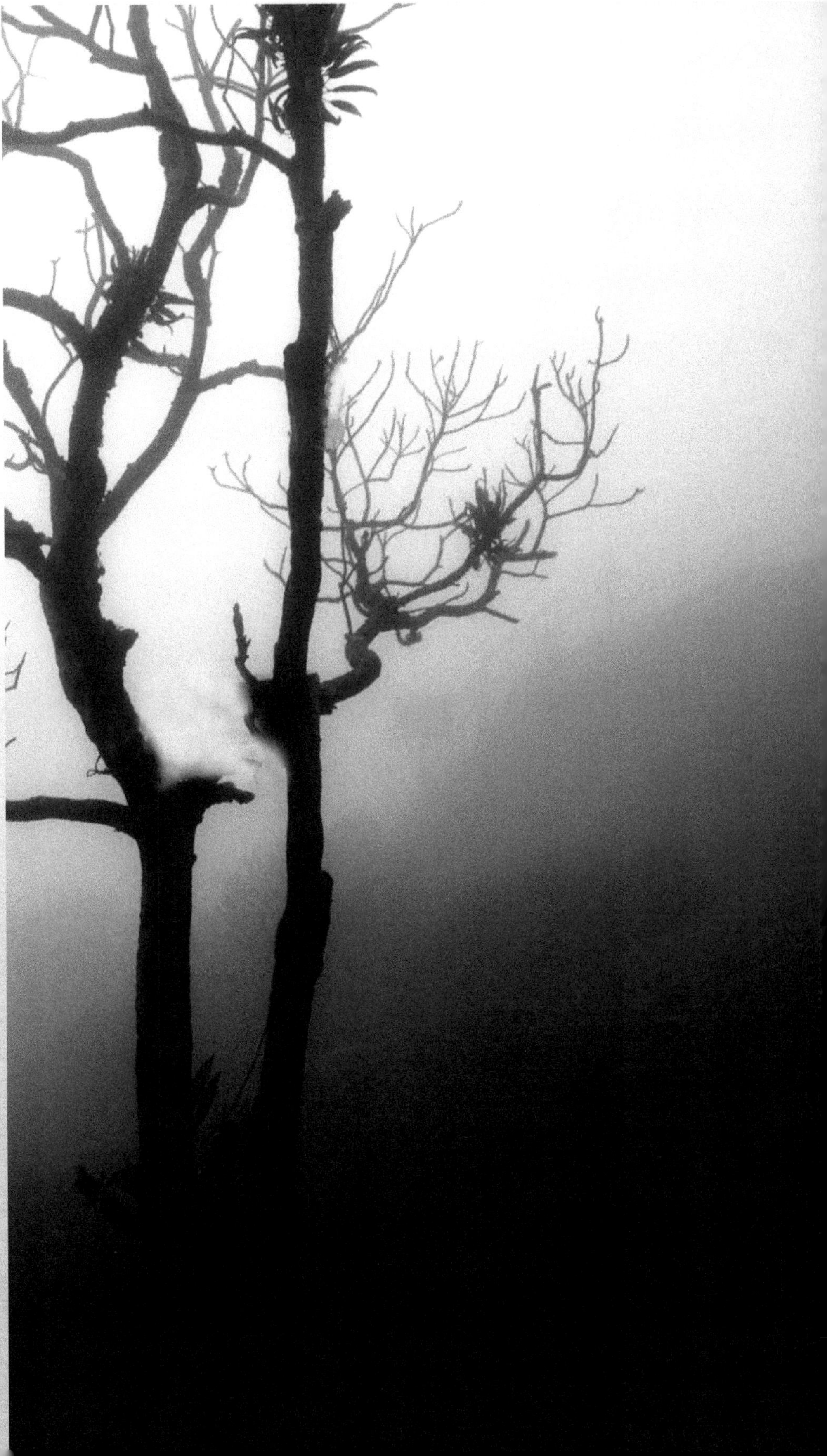

Darkness befell, forest rained torrential cascades
On precarious path of rocky cliff
That threatened to tumble the sky
I treaded forlornly an entire century
Beseeched others on the endless cycle of life
On horseback I once spanned the city
Passed this point where wailing demons flocked
Rose or fell with eyes blinded by floods
Swept away with the rolling pebbles I stepped on
Then toppled into a creek oozing blood
My corpse became leaves of grass bobbling downstream
I unfurled the moonbeams for a mat as the rain stopped
Millennium hence white flower dotted the hill

ODYSSEY UNTO SELF 8

ODYSSEY UNTO SELF 9

Unburdened my love for stalks of forest grass
I returned to the city for the love of all
Proffered my sweetness of life upon soul-baring rocks
Unfathomable fogs layered my being

A pebble, once my life
Sunlight streamed along the brook
An old reed pensive, as if
Asking how old you were

ODYSSEY UNTO SELF 10

ODYSSEY UNTO SELF (11)

Stepping forth, I felt the grass stirred
Perpetually I stepped unto empty-mindedness
The forest, as endless as dreams
Shrouded clouds far from sight

ODYSSEY UNTO SELF 12

Life unto life, day onto day
Into the lingering twilight, the forest leaves flew
Along the rocky cliff road
My stray footsteps imprinted forever the trace of exile

13 ODYSSEY UNTO SELF

Starting the return journey, latched your nón*
Wintry rain on the high pass to other worlds beyond

* Conical Vietnamese hat made of weaved bamboo palm leaves

ODYSSEY UNTO SELF
an afterthought

One late autumn morning of 2011, I received Teacher's email while sitting in a coffee bookstore in Dalat with only the following verses:

I am following the clouds aimlessly, horizons unknown. River sides, mountain caves, all are potential burial grounds. If there's a thread of predestiny, mayhaps we'll meet again, this life or next.

_ At the Hermitage of no-abode _

The email was sent last evening, meaning last night he was already wandering to the bus station, searching for any departure, to any destination reachable, undetermined. An odyssey of a monk without temple, without disciples, no place of arrival. To make such odyssey, aside from hidden ardor of self or of others, there must be an urge or a bind that is predestined. And the return was also a different urge or bind.

Unburdened my love for stalks of forest grass
Returned to the city for the love of all
Proffered my sweetness of life upon soul-baring rocks
Unfathomable fogs layered my being

Odyssey Unto Self, a string of 13 poems, was written after that journey. It opened with a return, and ended with an entreatment for another odyssey to begin. Stepping toward the end of the immeasurable road of life. The last two verses of this book of poetry brought us to a fitting close, but left un-closed our feelings of longing to be in harmony with the last ray of sunset or a fleeting starlight from far above. The tender entreatment was not a closing of the gate after the child return, but an opening of the back-yard gate leading to a path toward a horizon of infinite solitude.

Wintry rain on the high pass to other worlds beyond

Under the nebulous horizon, with starlight as beacon, and with the moonlight for a mat, then he slept only to begin his journey again the next morning, without knowing where he will be the next night, or if he will be 'fortunate' in finding a wind-screened shelter. It could be shrine on a desolate hillside; maybe behind the base of the colossal stone lion at the front gate of a temple where there was just enough space for him to lie unnoticed, watching other travelers passed by. A rest and a quick nap, rose at 3:00 AM, he collected his sparse belongings and continued on before the hurried city life returns again.

Life unto life, day onto day
Into the lingering twilight, the forest leaves flew...

The whiff of the lonesome distance beguiled, like the scent of wild, ripened fruits along the roads when hungry, like the bags of roasted peanuts given by a generous young man for his climb up the hillside 'because there is no one within a 6-mile radius', the young man said. Few bags of peanuts were enough for a day of ascending this lonesome hillside.

Afterward, sometimes he related his odyssey to me. I found it very challenging to write about these poems he wrote. They are of sun-scorched, dusty roads, of ominous sky laddered with dark clouds, of ravenous evening, of nights with immense longings of some homeland obscured. They are not of fanciful thoughts written on pristine white paper. This book of poetry, to me, is not for reading, understanding or writing about; only to be viewed, felt and conjured. I worry not about understanding the poems, but would be sadden if the readers can not conjure the landscape in

Since my tunic spread onto roads of dusty rain
Upon the harbor of emptiness I envisioned my past lived

Rain, sun, wind, dust. All the assiduous steps through forests and cities. To what end and for what pursuit? What did he seek from the stone baring its soul in the waning sunlight, from his leaning shadow upon the ledges of reeds fluttering with wistful yearnings? Where belonged a man, a stone, or the white, scattering reed flowers that blanketed the sky.

Rain, sun, wind, dust. *The world is full of countless aromatic grasses*[*]. In all directions grasses abound. A child pressed a cake into his hand, pointing to a tattered hut on the roadside: Mom said to give this to you. Humanity is as natural as the endless green, young grass. Green grasses and white reed flowers, whitened the solitary traveler's skylight with apprehension. In the midst of a city bustle, or before the endless green high plains, there are always moments of waywardness, of time seemingly fleeting. We want to search for something different to measure the distance between dream and reality. Some walks in blinding evening sunlight; some treads softly in dreams. Looking at the dusts beneath our feet, we are uncertain if they are homeland or homelessness.

Then toppled into a creek oozing blood
My corpse became leaves of grass bobbling downstream
I unfurled the moonbeams for a mat as the rain stopped
Millennium hence white flower dotted the hill

The moonlight appeared on the grass after the rain, as if spreading a mat of glittering velvet. Millennium hence, hearing stories of the Odyssey Unto Self, some will ask directly: To make such journey, to punish oneself, for what reason? Would all those aimless steps leave any trace upon the road-side pebbles. Perhaps not. Was there a dream left under the awning of his temporary resting place last night? And where would the high-plain drizzles wash this dream to? Then what is Odyssey Unto Self? It is not only a journey, but a journey without a beginning, without a destination; then surely it would have no return.

Starting the return journey, latched your nón[**]
Wintry rain on the high pass to other worlds beyond...

Hạnh Viên
Year of the Rat, Buddhist Calendar 2564

ODYSSEY UNTO SELF an afterthought

English translation
Nguyễn Phước Nguyên

---

[*] *Su Dongpo's poem*
[**] *Conical Vietnamese hat made of weaved bamboo palm leaves*

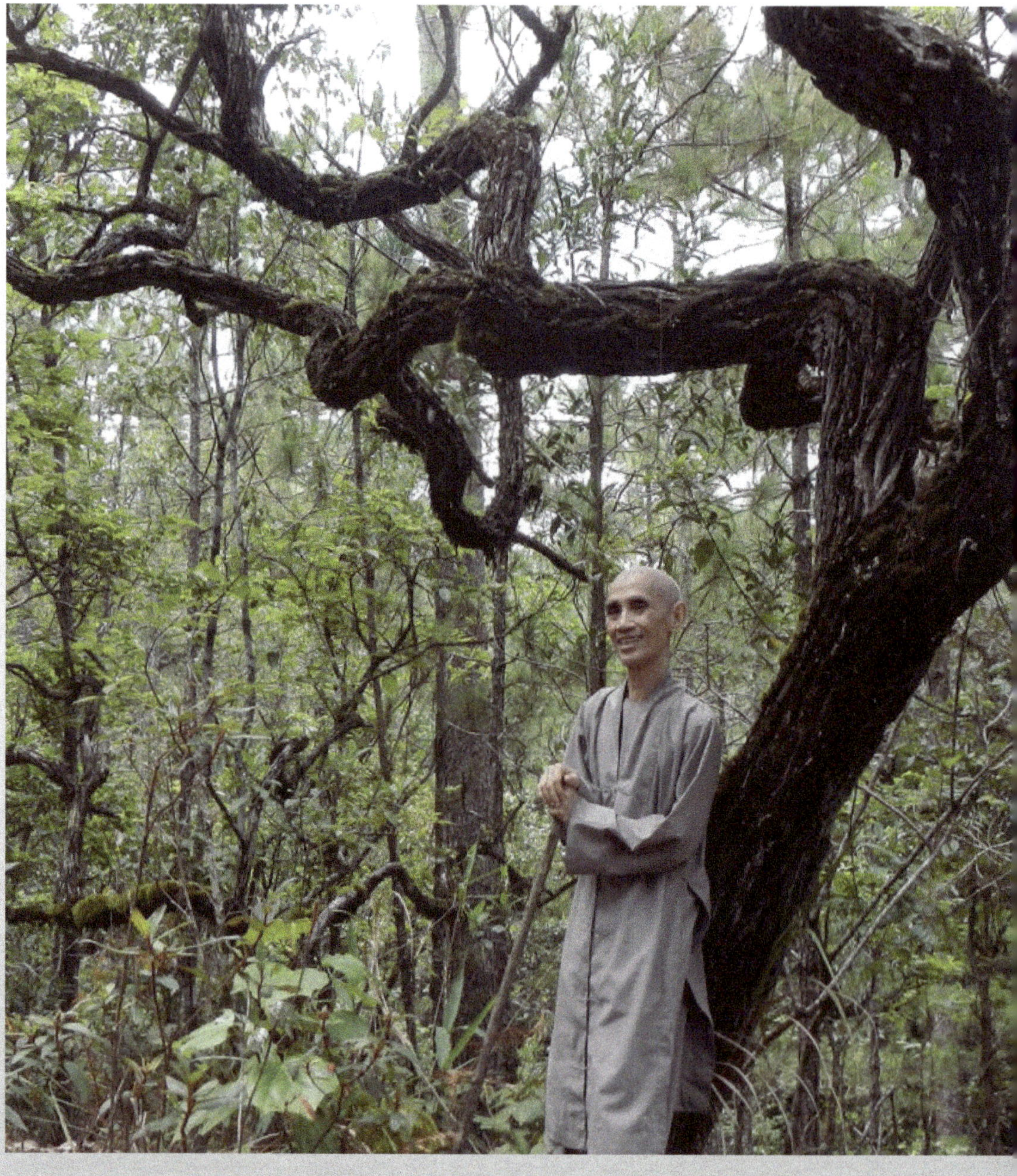

Une Odyssée Intérieure

UNE ODYSSEE INTERIEURE

Poème de Tuệ Sỹ

Une Odyssée Intérieure

UNE ODYSSÉE INTÉRIEURE

Poème de Tuệ Sỹ

1. UNE ODYSSEE INTERIEURE

La vacuité m'a saisi
Mon passé inonde le soleil qui s'estompe
Épris de mes jours d'errance
Je me blottis sous les étoiles
Qui s'impriment au fond de mes yeux

Harassé, sous le soleil je monte vers le sommet
Au crépuscule je ressens la douleur
des herbes effondrées
Ce qui n'était que fraicheur
Est devenu rives de solitude
Je suis seul, la montagne m'a cédé un coin
Au sommet
J'attends l'éternité

UNE ODYSSEE INTERIEURE 2.

3. UNE ODYSSEE INTERIEURE

Au sommet, un sanctuaire dédié aux âmes errantes
Mirages des lanternes vacillantes dans le ciel
L'ombre des vieux arbres s'étire dans le silence
Je médite en caressant une herbe

UNE ODYSSEE INTERIEURE

Infiniment, j'ai attendu
Ombre solitaire je foulais le temps
Sous le soleil, je suis une pierre
Caillou enveloppé des lames
du roseau pour couvrir mes peines

UNE ODYSSEE INTERIEURE 4.

5. UNE ODYSSEE INTERIEURE

D'où suis-je venu depuis l'aube du monde
Autour de moi, des feuilles ternies
J'entends le frisson de chaque souffle
Une âme flotte sur les roseaux

Au sommet, à perte de vue, la terre déployée
Forêts, nuages, immensité émeraude, plénitude
Depuis que ma tunique arpente les routes poussiéreuses
Au port de vacuité je perçois ma vie d'avant

UNE ODYSSEE INTERIEURE 6.

7. UNE ODYSSEE INTERIEURE

Chapeau bas - adieu
Au sommet, j'ai promis mon retour
Forêts de roseaux
Exilé depuis toujours
Ma vie après cette mort
Sur les chemins de poussières, sera toujours errante

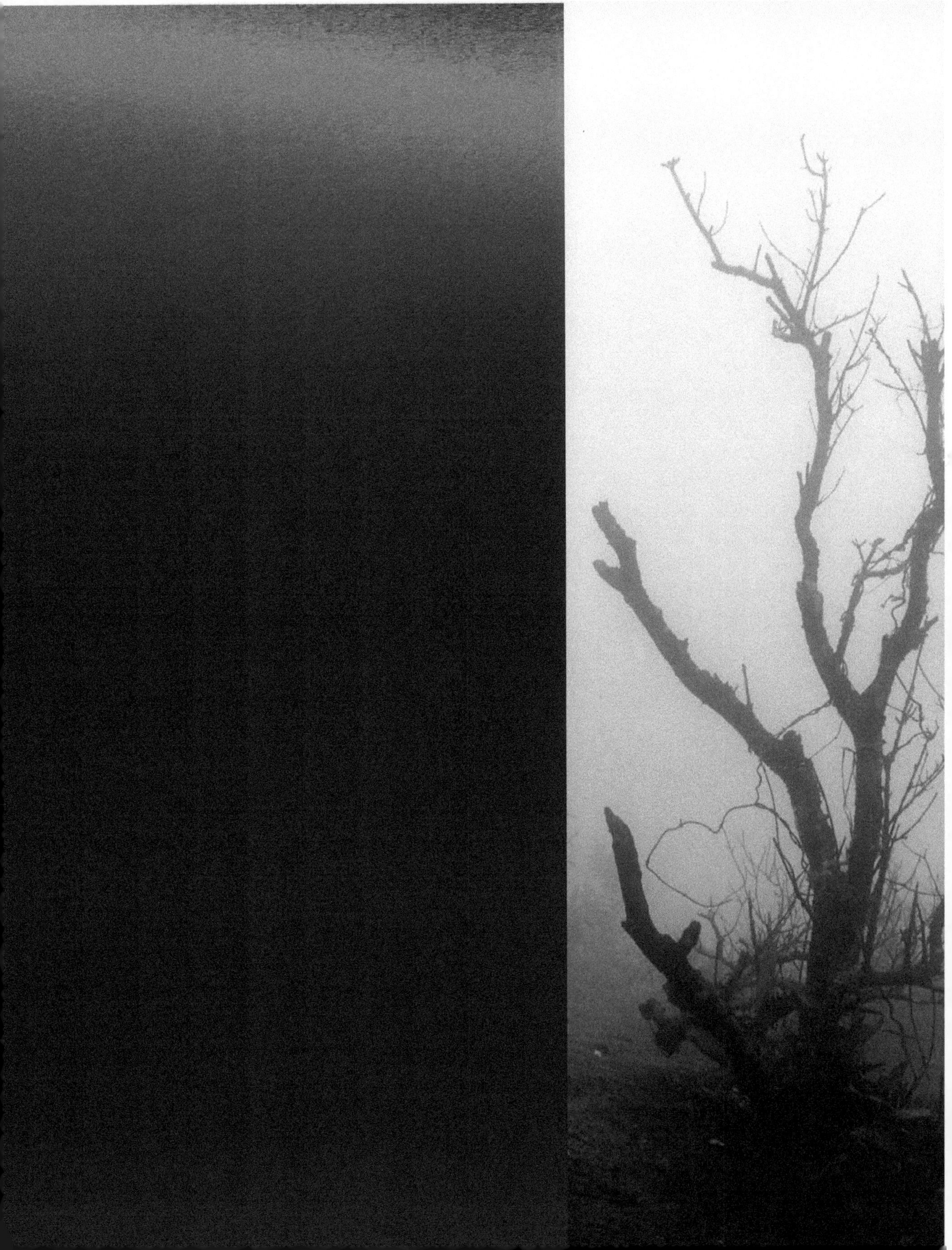

UNE ODYSSÉE INTERIEURE 8

L'obscurité tombe en torrents de cascades
Sur le sentier abrupt de la falaise
Le ciel s'est effondré
Accablé, j'ai arpenté un siècle entier
Implorant le cycle des vies sans fin
J'ai traversé la ville à cheval
Pénétré les lieux où les démons pullulent
Debout ou à terre les yeux aveuglés de larmes
Titubant sur les galets glissants
Emporté par un ruisseau de sang
Mon corps à terre devenu herbes flottantes
Je m'effondre sur un tapis de lune irisé de pluie
Seule, une fleur blanche fleurit millénaire après millénaires

9. UNE ODYSSEE INTERIEURE

Lesté de mon amour pour les herbes des forêts
Je suis retourné en ville par amour
Offrant mes doux miels aux rochers nus
Brouillards des épaisseurs insondables

Caillou, ma vie d'autrefois
La lumière du soleil ruisselle sur le torrent
Un vieux roseau pensif
Demande mon âge

UNE ODYSSEE INTERIEURE **10.**

11. UNE ODYSSEE INTERIEURE

Avançant, j'ai senti le frisson de l'herbe
Mon être s'est vidé de toutes ses scories
La forêt à l'infini telle un rêve
Les nuages à perte de vue

Vie après vie, jour après jour
Aveuglé par le crépuscule, les feuilles volent dans la forêt
J'ai marché sur le sentier abrupt
Mes pas d'exilé seront-ils imprimés à jamais?

UNE ODYSSEE INTERIEURE 12.

UNE ODYSSEE INTERIEURE 13.

Pour le voyage de retour, range ton nón lá *
Pluies glacées, le sommet est inhabité

* *Chapeau conique vietnamien, souvent en feuilles de latanier, mais toujours végétal*

UNE ODYSSEE INTERIEURE

En 2011, un matin de fin d'automne, j'ai reçu un courriel du Maître alors que j'étais assis dans une librairie-café à Dalat:

Je pars sans but, vers les nuages, des horizons inconnus. Longeant les rivières, les grottes de montagne, chaque endroit pourrait être un possible tombeau. S'il y a une prédestination, nous nous reverrons peut-être, dans cette vie ou la prochaine.

_ À l'Hermitage de non-abode _

L'e-mail avait été envoyé la veille au soir, c'est-à-dire la nuit dernière, Tue Sy partait de la gare routière, indéterminé, n'importe où. L'Odyssée d'un moine errant sans pagode, ni disciples, sans but. Pour s'aventurer ainsi, hors de soi et des autres, il doit y avoir un désir ou un terrain pré-destiné. Et le retour est aussi une résolution ou un lien d'un autre ordre.

Lesté de mon amour pour les herbes des forêts
Je suis retourné en ville par amour
Offrant mes doux miels aux rochers nus
Brouillards des épaisseurs insondables

Une Odyssée Intérieure : Ce sont 13 poèmes, écrits après ce voyage, qui s'ouvrent sur un retour, et se terminent sur une aspiration à un nouveau départ. Un pas vers la fin de la route de la vie. Les deux derniers vers nous projettent vers une fin acceptable, tout en laissant intacts nos sentiments d'être en harmonie avec le dernier rayon du soleil couchant ou la lumière d'une étoile furtive. La douce supplication n'est pas la fermeture de la porte après le retour de l'enfant, mais une ouverture dans l'arrière-cour menant vers un chemin sans fin d'une solitude infinie

Au sommet, froid de pluies, inhabité

Sous un horizon de brume, balisé par les étoiles, avec pour natte le clair de lune, il dormait; pour repartir le lendemain matin sans savoir où il serait la nuit suivante, ni s'il aurait la «chance» de trouver un abri. Ce pourrait être un sanctuaire sur une colline désolée; peut-être derrière un lion colossal en pierre, à la porte d'entrée d'un temple où il y avait juste assez d'espace pour passer inaperçu, en regardant le va et vient de la population. Le repos sera court, il se lève à 3 heures du matin, rassemble ses quelques affaires et continue avant que la vie agitée de la ville ne revienne.

Vie après vie, jour après jour
Aveuglé par le crépuscule, les feuilles volent dans la forêt

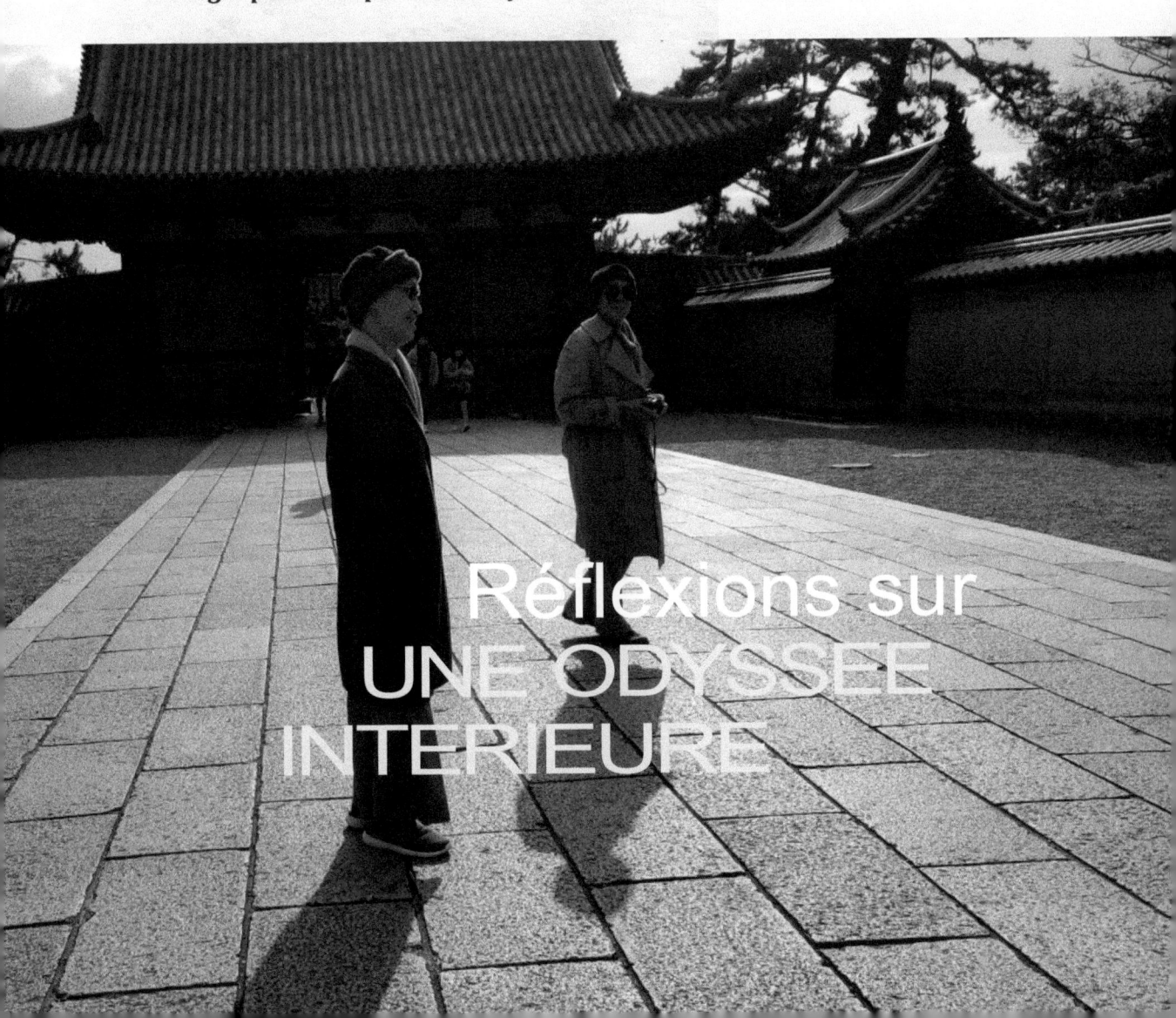

Réflexions sur UNE ODYSSEE INTERIEURE

Tue Sy est séduit par sa marche en solitaire: le long des routes, l'odeur des fruits sauvages à maturité aiguisent la faim, un jeune homme lui offre quelques pochettes de cacahuètes grillés pour la montée de la journée - il n'y a personne à 10 km à la ronde lui avait-il dit. Quelques pochettes d'arachides ont suffi pour la journée.

Par la suite, il me parlait parfois de son odyssée. Ce fut pour moi très difficile d'écrire sur ces poèmes. Les routes étaient brûlantes de soleil, poussiéreuses, le ciel souvent menaçant, les soirées où il était affamé, ses nuits remplies de désirs obscurs. Ce ne sont absolument pas des fantaisies écrites sur du papier immaculé. Ce livret de poèmes, pour moi, n'est pas destiné à être lu, compris ou écrit, il doit être vu, ressenti et conjuré. Il ne s'agit pas de simplement comprendre les poèmes, néanmoins je serais triste si les lecteurs n'étaient pas touchés par les paysages

Depuis que ma tunique arpente les routes poussiéreuses
Au port de vacuité je perçois ma vie d'avant

Pluie, soleil, vent, poussière. Toutes ces étapes à travers les forêts et les villes. À quelle fin et pourquoi? Que trouve-t'il dans ses aspirations nostalgiques, à cette pierre qui découvre son être au soleil déclinant, à son ombre penchée sur les lames des roseaux? Nous appartenons à ce monde de pierres et de fleurs blanches des roseaux dispersées qui s'épandent au firmament...

Pluie, soleil, vent, poussière. *Le monde regorge d'herbes fragrantes**. Partout les herbes abondent... Sur le bord de la route, un enfant lui donne un gâteau, devant une hutte délabrée: Maman m'a dit de vous le donner. L'humanité est aussi naturelle que la jeune herbe verte ou les fleurs blanches des roseaux. Elles en sont les témoins et réconfortent le voyageur solitaire. Au milieu de l'agitation urbaine, ou devant les hautes plaines vertes sans fin, il y a toujours des moments de caprices, un temps apparemment éphémère. Nous recherchons des espaces différents pour mesurer la distance entre le rêve et la réalité. Quelques promenades sous le soleil aveuglant du soir; certains marchent doucement dans leurs rêves. En regardant la poussière sous nos pieds, nous ne savons pas d'où elle vient.

Réflexions sur UNE ODYSSEE INTÉRIEURE

Glissant sur les galets
Emporté par un ruisseau de sang
Mon corps à terre devenu herbes flottantes
Je m'effondre sur un tapis de lune irisé de pluie
Seule, une fleur blanche fleurit millénaire après millénaires

Le clair de lune apparaît sur l'herbe après la pluie, tel un tapis de velours scintillant. Mille ans donc, en écoutant Une Odyssée Intérieure, certains demanderont: pourquoi aire un tel voyage, pour se punir ou quelle autre raison? Tous ces pas sans but laisseront-ils une trace sur les cailloux au bord de la route? Peut-être pas. Quel rêve a été abandonné sous l'auvent temporaire de la nuit dernière. Et comment les bruines douloureuses peuvent-elles chasser ce rêve? Alors qu'est-ce que cette Odyssée Intérieure? Sûrement pas qu'un voyage. Un voyage sans commencement et sans destination ; il n'y aura pas de retour.

Pour le voyage de retour, range ton nón lá[**]
Au sommet, froid de pluies, inhabité

Hạnh Viên
Année du Rat, Calendrier Bouddhiste 2564

Traduction en Français
Dominique de Miscault

---

[*] *Poème de Su Dongpo*
[**] *Chapeau conique Vietnamien, souvent en feuilles de latanier, mais toujours végétal*

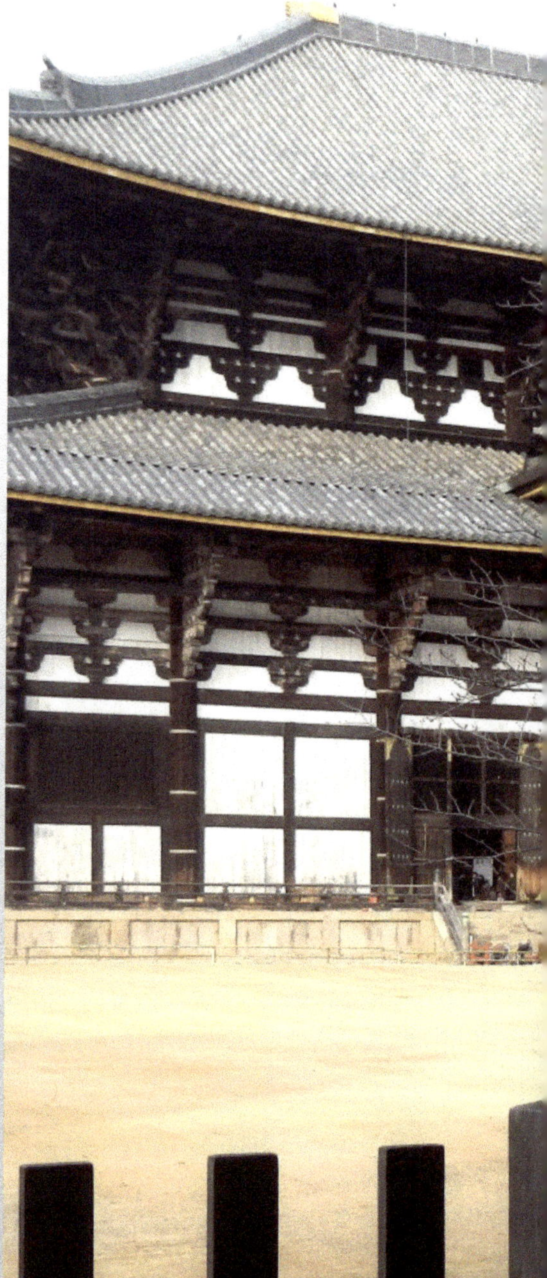

千里独行

IV. Senri okko
千里独行

Tuệ Sỹ 詩

千里独行

Senridokkoo

Tuệ Sỹ 詩

Senridokkoo

Kuushin no　kyosho ni modori
Irihi ni　kako afureta kanji
Hooroo no hibi　imada shitawashiki
Han'ya no ensei　mezoko ni atsumari

千里独行

一

空心の　居所に戻り
落日に　過去溢れた感じ
放浪の日々　未だ慕わしき
半夜の遠星　目底に集まり

Senri dokkoo

Tooge no hizashi o fumi'ayumi
Sha'yoo to tomo ni sookon itami o kanji
Gensho wa aikyoo na sugatazakari
Totsujo kutsugaeshi jakuryoo no kishi
Ima wa potsu'nen to yamakado gotoki
Sennen tatte teppen ni machidooshii

千里独行

二

峠の日差しを　踏み歩み
斜陽とともに　草魂傷みを感じ
原初は　愛嬌な姿盛り
突如覆し　寂廖の岸
今はぽつねんと　山角如き
千年経って　天辺に待ち遠しい

Senridokkoo

Tooge no hotori ni   mu'enbotoke no hokora
Gen'ei no sora ni   miekakure no tomoshibi
Koju ni   kurayami ga shigeri
Nogusa idaite   mukyoo tadori

千里独行

三

峠の辺(ほと)りに　無縁仏の祠(ほこら)
幻影(げんえい)の空に　見え隠れの灯火
古樹(こじゅ)に　暗闇が繁り
野草(のぐさ)抱いて　夢境(むきょう)辿り

Senridokkoo

Tsukihatete matte'ita   suusennen nari
Tasogare o fumu   kodoku na hito no kage
Wa ga sekkon o   yookoo ni hoshi
Ashigaki idaite   kanashisa kakushi

千里独行

四

尽き果てて待っていた　数千年也(なり)
黄昏(たそがれ)を踏む　孤独な人の影
我が石魂(せっこん)を　陽光に乾(ほ)し
葦垣(あしがき)抱いて　哀しさ隠し

Senridokkoo

Kookoo no tabi yori   ware izuko ni
Mawari no juyoo   moo iro asetari
Koki no yure o   totsujo ni kanji
Ashimure ni   honoka na tarebito no tamashii

千里独行

　　五

鴻荒(こうこう)の度より　我(われ)何処(いずこ)に
周りの樹葉(じゅよう)　もう色褪(いろあ)せたり
呼気(こき)の揺れを　突如に感じ
葦群(あしむれ)に　ほのかな誰人(たれびと)の魂

Senri dokkoo

Tooge no teppen ni   happoo o mi
Mori kumo shinryoku ni   shizukesa kagiri naki
Ujin no michi ni   koromojiki toki yori
Kuu no kishi ni   zenshin kaisoo shi keri

千里独行

六

峠の頂辺(てっぺん)に　八方を見
森雲深緑(もりぐもしんりょく)に　静けさ限りなき
雨塵(うじん)のみちに　衣敷(ころもじ)き時より
空(くう)の岸に　前身(ぜんしん)回想しけり

Senridokkoo

Kasa o katamuke　kaeri no aisatsu
Tooge no ochiai ni　ashibara to machiau
Chinrin ga　gensho no tabi yori
Raise mo mata　michichiri to sasurai

千里独行

七

笠を傾け　帰りの挨拶
峠の落ち合いに　葦原と待ち合う
沈淪が　原初の度より
来世もまた　道塵と流離い

Senri Okkoo

Senridokkoo

Yami orite　yama'ame no teppoomizu
Chuu ni uku michi　ishigake ga oshikakari
Yo o shinobi no inki ga　seiki o oyobi
Izanaite　hitasura rinne no do ni
Umakakemawari　i'nishi bi no machi
Toorikake ni　kimi ga mure nashite naki
Meshii mo demizu to　agari sagattari
Ashifumi ni　shareki tomo korobi nagaretari
Soshite taore　izumi wa chi ni afuredashi
Kusaba no mi ga　dakuboku kudari
Ame agari machi　tsuki o goza ni shi
Sennen nochi　shiroi hana　oka ni saki

千里独行

Senridokkoo

千里独行　八

闇おりて　山雨（やまあめ）の鉄砲水
宙に浮く路（みち）　石崖が押し掛かり
世を忍びの陰鬼（いんき）が　世紀を及び
誘（いざな）いて　ひたすら輪廻（りんね）の処（ど）に
馬駆け回り　往（いに）し日の街
通りかけに　鬼魅（きみ）が群れなして泣き
盲（めしい）も出水（でみず）と　上がり下がったり
足踏みに　砂礫（しゃれき）とも転び流れたり
そして倒れ　泉（いずみ）は血に溢れ出し
草葉（くさば）の身が　だくぼく降り
雨上がり待ち　月を茣蓙（ござ）にし
千年後（のち）　白い花　丘に咲き

Senri ciokkoo

Yamagusa no　koi o nokoshi
Seken'ai motome ni　machi modori
Sekkonboshi ni　koozui jinsei o sasage
Haruka na too'nada ni　shimo ikue

千里独行

九

山草(やまぐさ)の　恋を残し
世間愛(せけんあい)求めに　都会(まち)戻り
石魂(せっこん)乾(ぼ)しに　香蕊人生を捧げ
遥かな遠灘(とおなだ)に　霜幾重(いくえ)

Senri dokkoo

Hitotoki ga   sazare ishi no mi
Yookoo nagarete   izumi zoi
Oi'ashi ga   yuushi to shi
Taregashi ni   toshi o toi

千里独行

十

ひと時が　さざれ石の身(み)
陽光(ようこう)流れて　泉沿い
老い葦が　憂思(ゆうし)とし
誰某(たれがし)に　歳を問い

Senridokkoo

Hito'ayumi ni　kusa'yure o kanji
Tsuzukete ayumeba　kokoro mo kuu nari
Haruka na mori ga　mugen gotoki
Kumokemuri　kasanatte tsunagari

千里独行

十一

一歩みに　草揺れを感じ
続けて歩めば　心も空成り
遥かな森が　夢幻如き
雲煙　重なって繋がり

Senridokkoo

Mi wa mi ni   hi wa hi ni tsuzuki
Mori no man'yoo ga   yo'ei ni tobichirashi
Ishigake no komichi ni   tadotte ayumi
Imada ni   kokoro yorube nashi no hibi

千里独行

十二

身(み)は身に　日(ひ)は日に続き
森の万葉(まんよう)が　余映(よえい)に飛び散らし
石崖の古路(こみち)に　辿って歩み
未(いま)だに　心寄る方(よるべ)なしの日々

Senridokkoo

千里独行

十三

帰路(きろ)に　笠紐(かさひも)を結んでしっかり
高い峠冷たい雨　人の世(よ)もなし

Kiro ni　kasahimo o musunde shikkari
Takai tooge tsumetai ame　hito no yo mo nashi

Senridokkoo ni atotsugu

千里独行に跡継ぐ

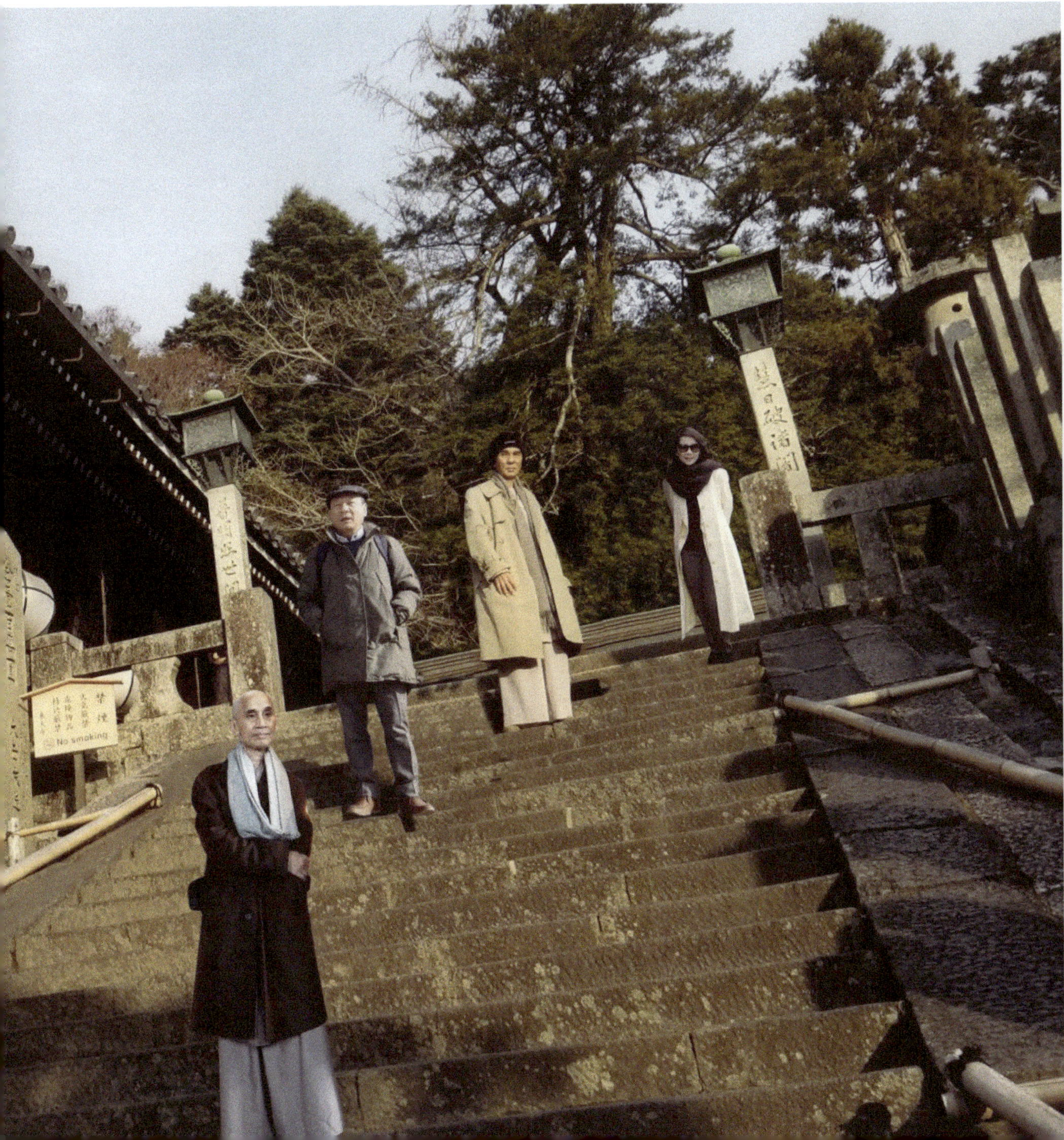
慧日破諸闇
禁煙
No smoking

2011年晩秋のとある朝、ダラットの本屋の喫茶コーナーにいた時、老師から数行のEメールを受け取った。

　　　　私は雲と放浪し、行き先未定。河岸山谷、どこも死骸置き
　　　　になろう。まだ縁が残れば再会の機を、今世か来世の何れ。
　　　　　　　　　　　　　　　　　　　　　　　　是岸庵無住処

メールは前日の夕方に送信され、というのはすでに前夜から老師はバスターミナルをうろつき、行く先を定めぬ旅にふさわしい便を探していたことであろう。寺もなく、侍従もない修行者の旅路は行き先もない。そのような旅立ちは、公私ともの心情以外には元々衝動的また必然的なものであり、そして戻るときにもまた別の衝動や必然によるものである。

　　　　山草の　恋を残し
　　　　世間愛求めに　都会戻り
　　　　石魂乾しに　香蕊人生を捧げ
　　　　遥かな遠灘に　霜幾重

千里独行、13綴りの連詩はその旅を終えた後に書き下ろしたものである。この連詩は帰路にはじまり、そして結びを次の旅立ちへの餞言葉として、遥か長き夢のような人生をさらに歩んでゆく。詩集を結ぶはずの最後2行はその役割を果たせず、憂鬱な情念は憂鬱な情念のままに、夕日にも天の果ての遠星にも連なっていく。親しみな言葉は浮浪児が帰郷後に門を静かに閉める代わりに、また悠遠の彼方を導くしるべとなるだろう

　　　　高い峠　冷たい雨　人の世もなし

そのまぼろしの彼方、星影が照らす道のり、草むらの月あかりを茣蓙にして休み、再び早朝から旅の続き、またその夜の宿りも定めず、運良く無風の寝床を見つけるのやら。時には峠辺りの無縁仏の祠、ある時は寺山門の石獅子の裏に人目隠しほどの小さな穴。脚休みと一眠りしてまた朝3時に起き清掃して、都会に騒がしい新しい日を返して旅の続きをし。

　　　　身は身に　日は日に続き
　　　　森の万葉が　余映に飛び散らし

千里の荒寥たる味はどこまでも幻惑し、空腹時の道端に熟した果実の匂いのよう。または夕刻に峠越え前にある親切な青年から数袋の煎りピーナッツを手渡され、告げられる。「半径10キロは民家なし」。ピーナッツ数袋はこの人気無し峠を通過するには十分であろう。

後に時々旅の話を聴くことがあり、益々この連詩を写実的批評することは極めて難しいと感じている。埃っぽく酷しい日射し、暗雲が垂れ込めた空、空腹の夕べ、消えていた故郷を想いおこす長い夜…、それらは真っ白な紙に幻想を綴るためのものではない。私にとってこの詩集は、読み、理解、批評するためではなく、読んで、感じてそして想像するためのものである。詩を読むとき、理解しようとするよりも詩のなかに描いた景色を想像してほしいものである。

　　　　雨塵のみちに　衣敷き時より
　　　　空の岸に　前身回想しけり

雨、日射し、風、ほこり、そして山や街に何のため何を探しに歩を進めるのか？石魂乾しの黄昏色、または葦垣に揺れている人影の遠地、その心境に何が見いだされるだろう？人間の、石の、葦の綿毛が風とともに四方に散りばりの何処に…

日射し、ほこり、風、雨。「天涯何處無芳草」*僻地八百路に何処も芳草あり。突如小さな子が「母からです」と言い、片手は道沿いに倒れそうな小屋を指して老師の手にケーキ一つを押しつけた。人間の情けは、広がる若草の如くに自然発生するものだ。野原の白い葦綿毛は、孤独の空を白く染めている。都会の車馬の間を歩むときも、あるいは緑の草原を歩むときも、漂泊の思いが突然襲い、夢幻の日々を感じる。何ものかを目指して訪ねて行き、夢実両岸の幅を測ろうと、斜陽のなかに歩む人、浮遊の夢のなかに歩む者。足下のほこりを見てここは他処か故里かの何れか不知。

　　　　そして倒れ　泉は血に溢れ出し
　　　　草葉の身が　　だくぼく降り
　　　　雨上がり待ち　月を莫蓙にし
　　　　千年後　白い花　丘に咲き

雨後の月光は草むらにきらきら、錦莫蓙の如き広がり。

千年後…。千里独行を聞いた真面目な方はこう問うだろう。「何のため自分を苦しめる旅をするのだろう？　行き先定めずの歩みは道端の砂礫に何か痕残しできたのだろうか？　多分ないよね、あるにしても昨夜泊まった庇に夢を残していたが、それも高原の雨が何処へ連れていてしまっただろう。」

然も千里独行とは？一度の旅に限らず。出発のない旅、そして行き先定めない旅、だから到達地のない旅は帰還もなし。

　　　　帰路に　笠紐を結んでしっかり
　　　　高い峠冷たい雨　人の世もなし

　　　　　　　　　　　ハイン・ヴィエン（Hạnh Viên 杏園）
　　　　　　　　　　　仏暦2564 庚子年夏季

和訳　ブイ・チ・トルン
Bùi Chí Trung

_____

*蘇東坡の詩

千里独行

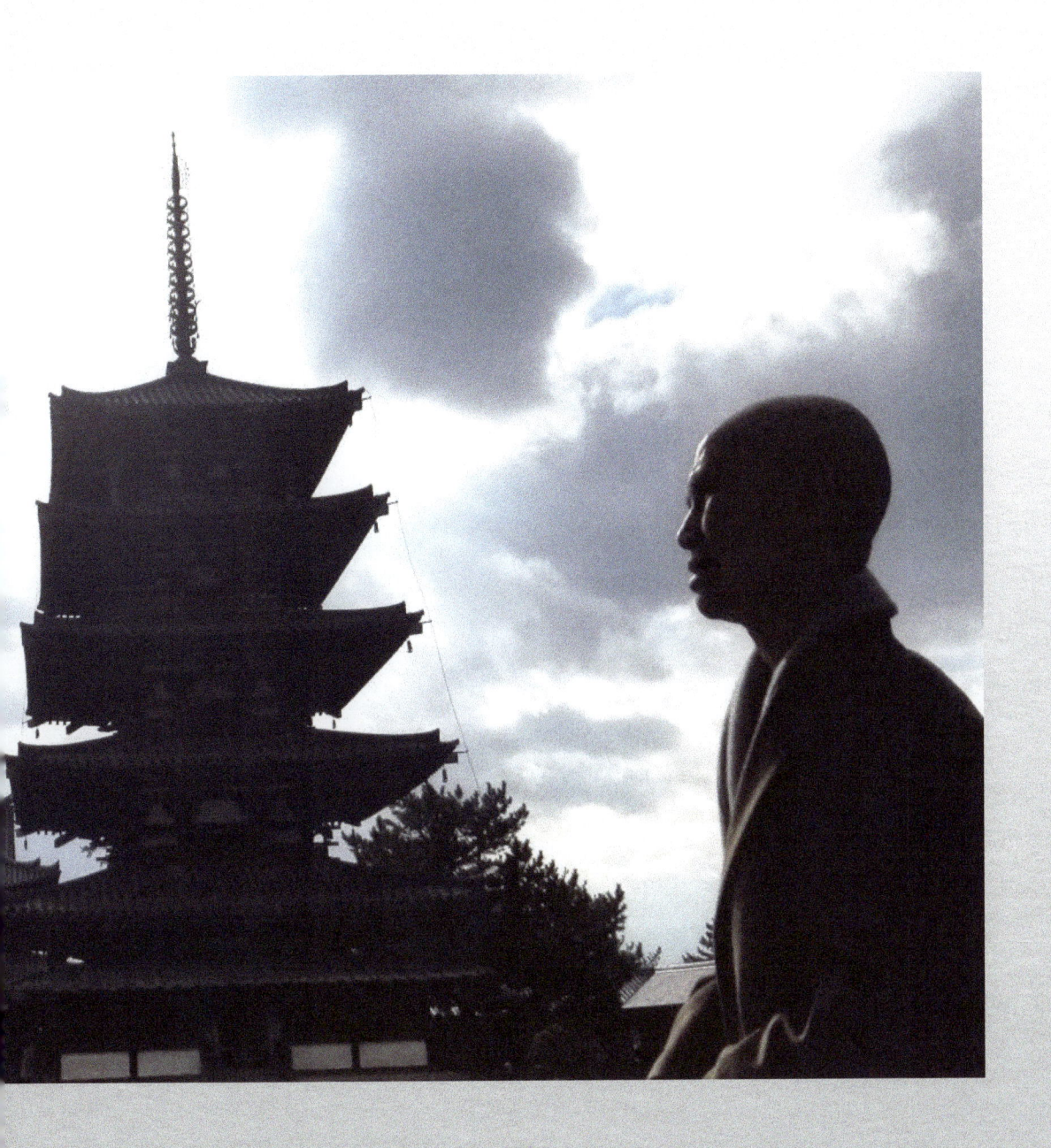

過去心不可得現在心不可得未來心不可得

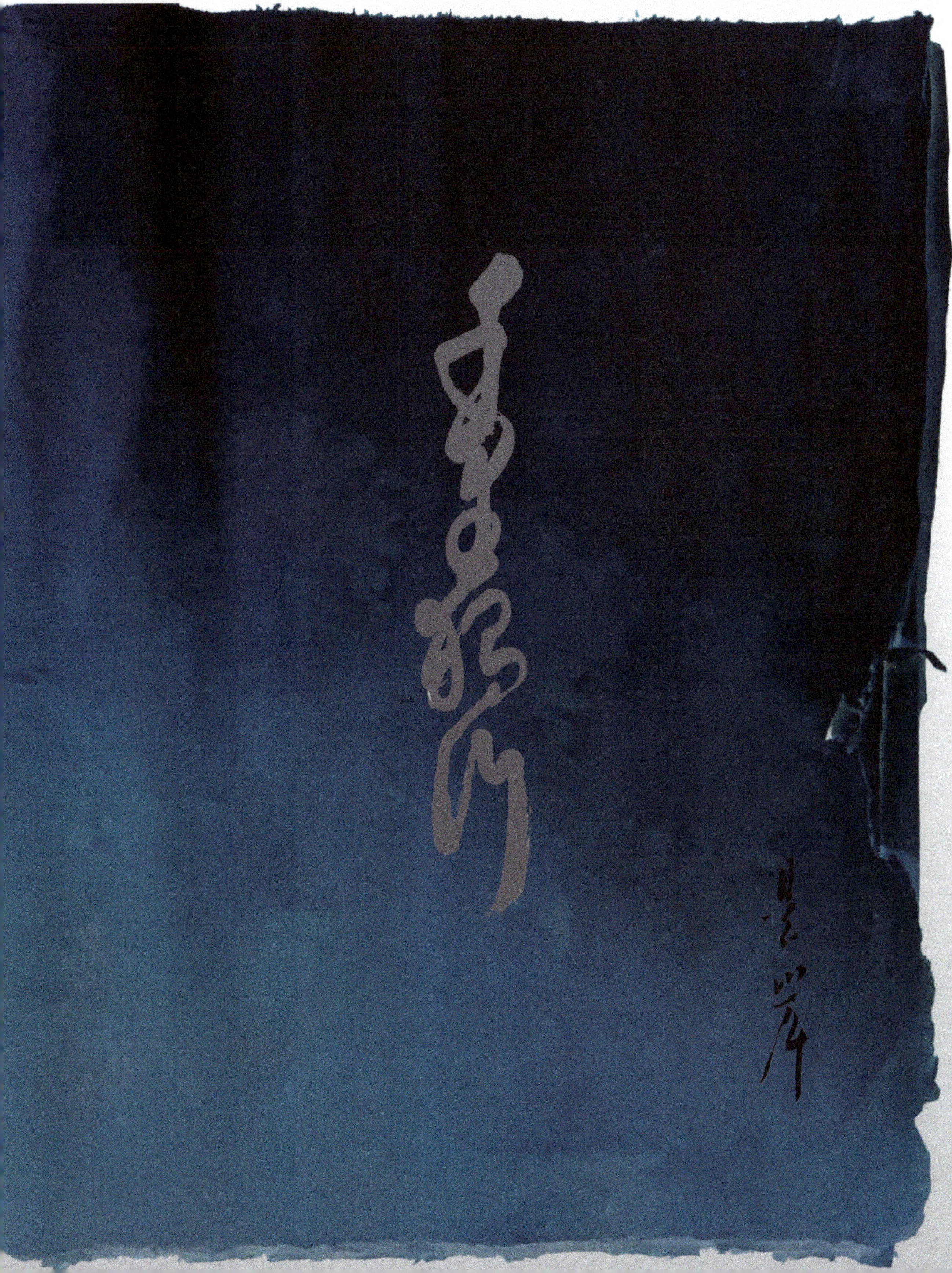

千里独行

Senridokkoo

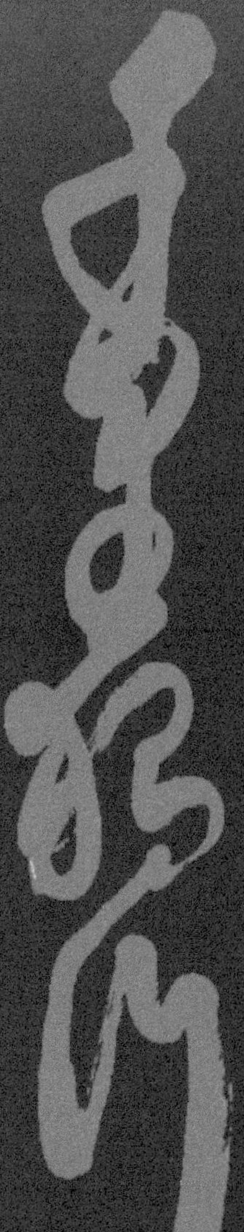

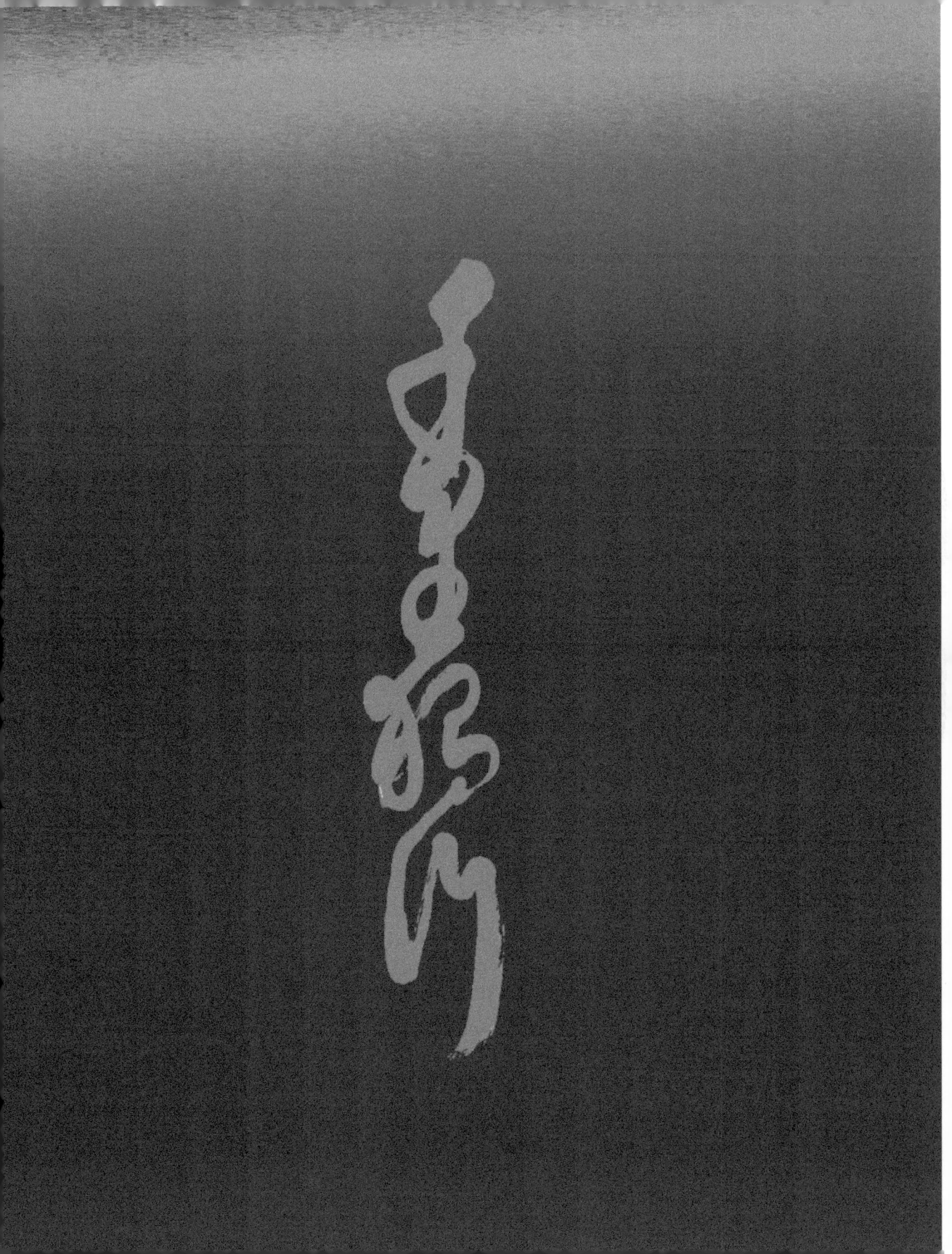

長岸

Milton Keynes UK
Ingram Content Group UK Ltd.
UKHW050028250924
448735UK00017B/228

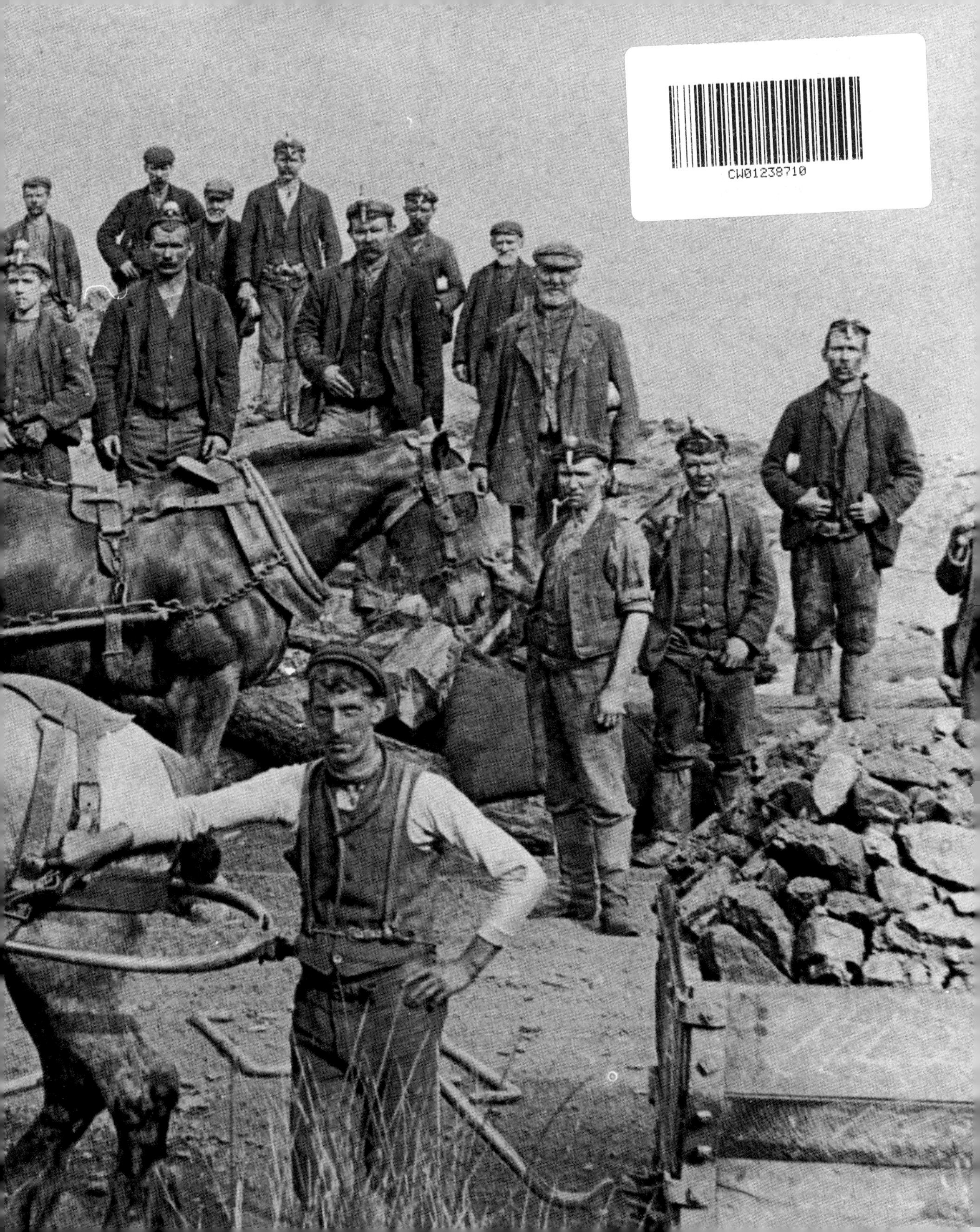

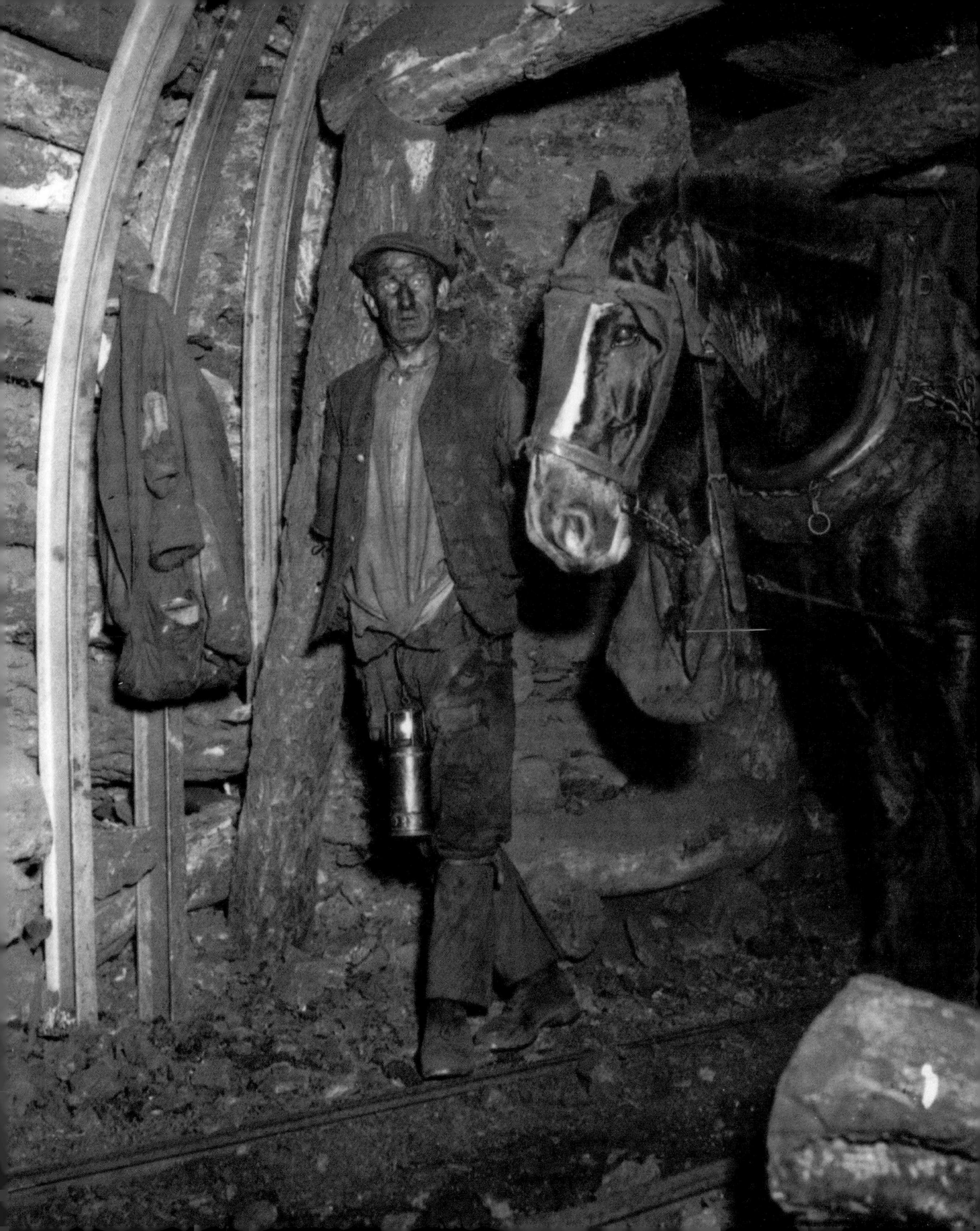

Harnessed

COLLIERY HORSES IN WALES

Joe Williams
March '11

First published in 2008 by Amgueddfa Cymru – National Museum Wales,
Cathays Park, Cardiff, CF10 3NP, Wales.
www.museumwales.ac.uk

© National Museum of Wales

ISBN 978-0-7200-0591-2

Editing and production: Mari Gordon
Design: Mo-Design
Printed by: Gomer Press

Welsh-language edition available, *Cyfaill neu gaethwas? Ceffylau'r pyllau glo*
ISBN 978-0-7200-0590-5

All rights reserved. No part of this publication may be reproduced, stored in a retrieval system or transmitted in any form or by any means, electrical, mechanical or otherwise, without prior permission in writing from Amgueddfa Cymru – National Museum Wales, the copyright owner(s) or as expressly permitted by law. Enquiries should be sent to the Publications Department, National Museum Cardiff, Cardiff CF10 3NP.

All images are © National Museum of Wales unless stated otherwise.

The author's moral rights have been asserted.

Cover photo: 'Able' of Glyncorrwg Colliery – second place in Merthyr Horse Show, June 1955
Inside front cover: Hauliers, horses and drams at Ton Level, Ton Pentre
Title page: A horse and haulier, probably at Penallta colliery, about 1940
Inside back cover: Rearing horses for colliery use

Environmental statement:
The fibre for this paper is virgin wood fibre, mainly from Austria but also from Brazil, Canada, Portugal, Spain and Sweden. The pulp is bleached using mainly a Totally Chlorine Free (TCF) process but some is bleached using an Elemental Chlorine Free (ECF) process. This material can be disposed of by recycling, incineration for energy recovery or is biodegradable. It is produced at a mill that is certified to the ISO14001 environmental management standard and certified to the EMAS environmental management standard (number A-S-000009).

Harnessed

COLLIERY HORSES IN WALES

By Ceri Thompson

NATIONAL MUSEUM WALES BOOKS

Above: Eileen Watson painting 'Tinker'
Right: the finished painting

Acknowledgments

Tony Barlow, Andy Brown, Vince Court, Cyfarthfa Castle Museum, Ivor Davies, Einion Evans, Glamorgan Record Office, George Heard, Len Howell, Paul Jackson, Paul Meredith, National Coal Mining Museum for England, Mel Payne, Bill Richards, Gareth Salway, Andrew Williams, Keith Williams.

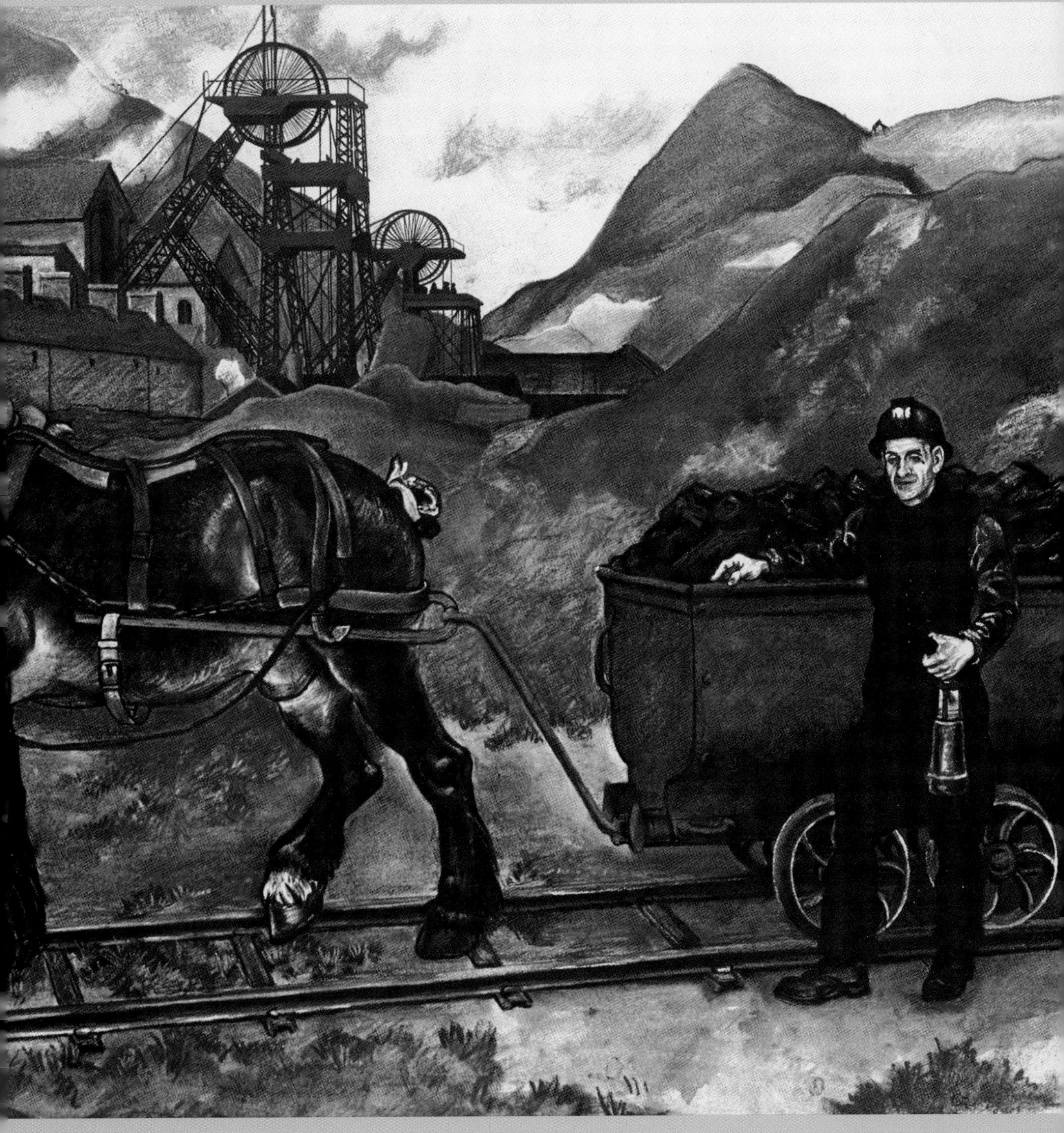

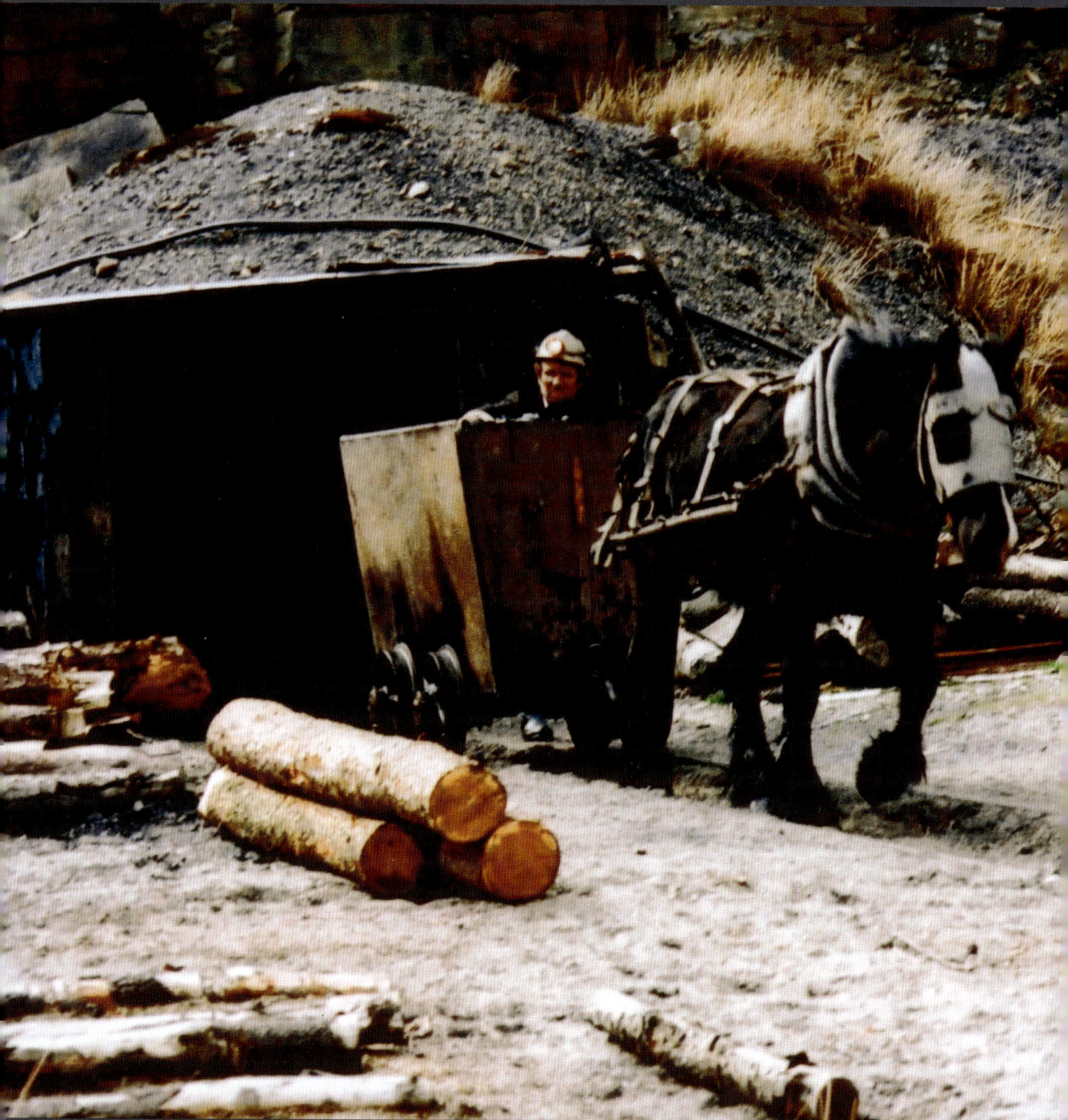

Contents

Introduction	10
Colliery horses or pit ponies?	12
Getting them underground	16
Life in the colliery	22
Work	30
Cruelty in secret places?	36
Danger, injuries and death	42
Pit horses and politics	48
High days and holidays	52
Horses at Big Pit	60
The end of the road	64
Glossary	70
Further reading	71

'Robbie', possibly Britain's last working colliery horse, at Pant y Gasseg Mine, about 1999
(Photo courtesy of Paul Jackson)

Introduction

Wretched, blind pit ponies
Ralph Hodgson, *The Bells of Heaven*, 1917

They are treated as willing pets rather than slaves.
Lord Dorchester, *Exhibition of Colliery Horses*, 1938

Horses have been closely connected with coal mining since the early days of the industry. They have been used to transport coal from the collieries to the customer, to power winding and pumping engines and, most importantly, to move coal from the coalface to the shaft. In 1878, the RSPCA calculated that there were over 200,000 at work in British mines.

Although they were essential for the production of coal before the introduction of mechanized haulage, the use of horses in the coal industry has often been highly controversial. The coal owners argued that they were vital in the economic process of winning coal, while animal lovers regarded their use as inhumane.

In between these opposing sides were the mineworkers, who might have felt sympathy for these animals. However, they could turn a blind eye to any callousness, or even be cruel themselves, if their pay packets were under threat.

Whether a 'willing pet' or 'wretched pit pony', the colliery horse shared the same conditions and dangers as the coalminer; they were used as a propaganda tool by both sides during industrial disputes, and they died in their hundreds from mistreatment, accident and explosion. The ultimate use for many of these four-legged mineworkers was as dog food – but without them the industrial revolution would have failed.

This book commemorates their lives.

Above: A cartoon from *Coal News*, 1940s
Right: A handler with horses, Penallta Colliery, about 1940

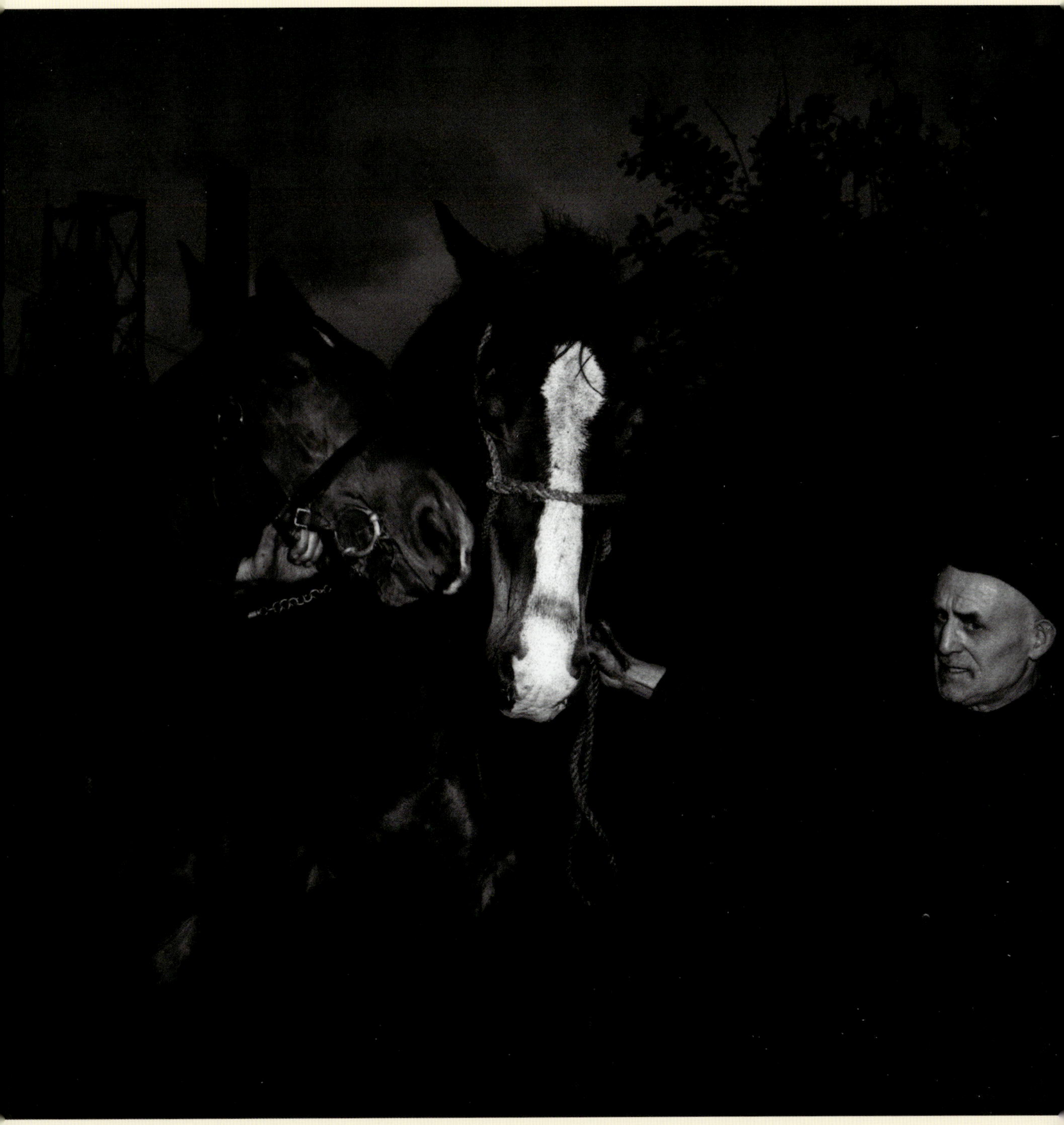

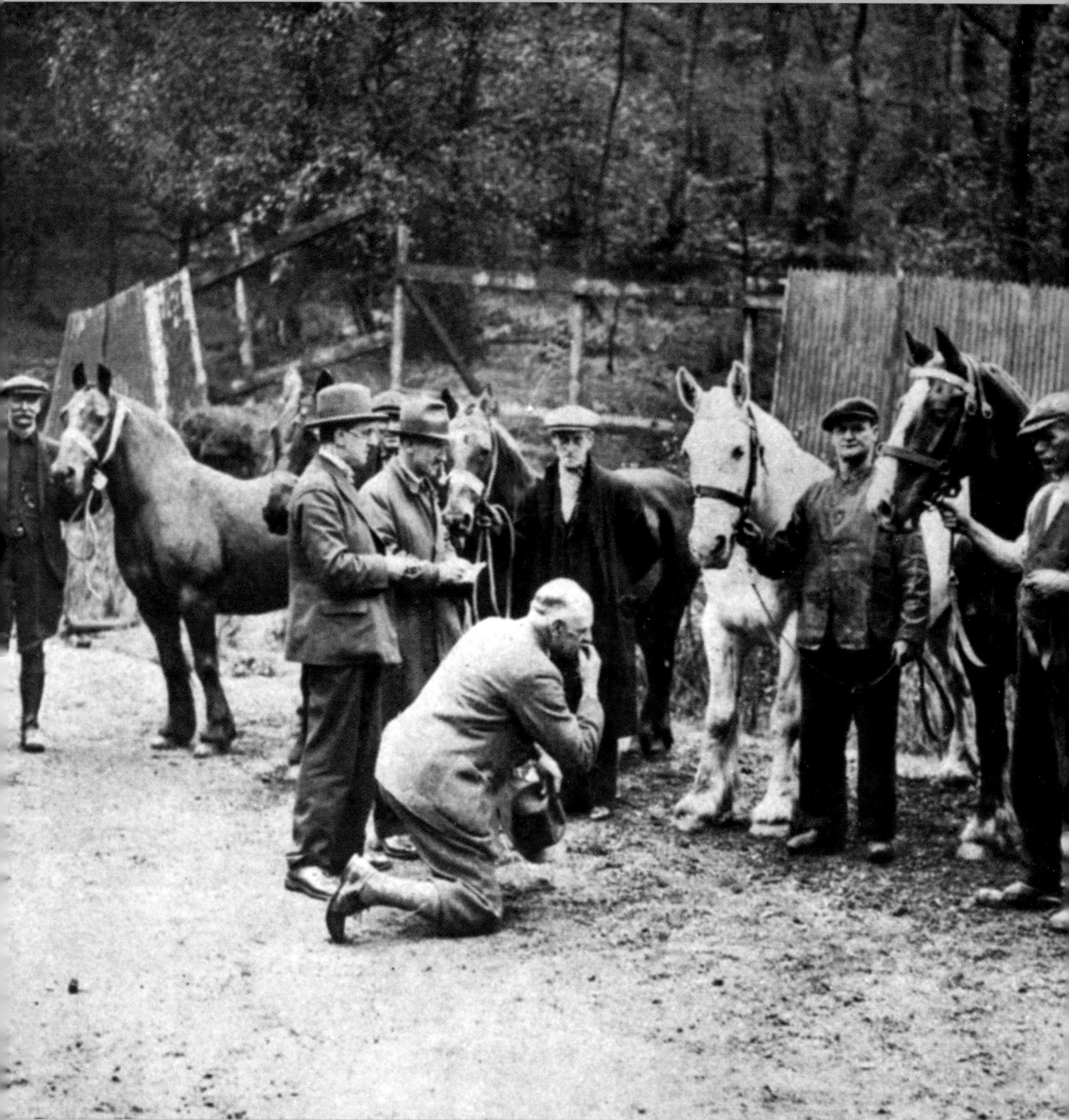

Colliery horses or pit ponies?

> Not ponies in Wales, we exported them to lesser coalfields.
> **Philip Weekes, Director of the South Wales Coalfield, 1973-1984**

Although often referred to as 'pit ponies' by the general public, most of the animals used in Welsh collieries were actually horses.

> I was always scared of them really. As they were coming along the roads I had it in my mind where was the nearest manhole, because there wasn't much room. They were big! You had great respect for them when they were on the move.
> **George Heard, Penallta Colliery, 1944-5**

Left: Horses being selected for colliery work in 1930
Above: 'Gilbert', who worked for 17 years underground at Lewis Merthyr Colliery

Hauling coal at Britannic Colliery, May 1931

The particular geology of the Welsh steam coal seams meant that they were relatively easy to cut and the coal usually fell out in large, irregular blocks. These blocks needed a large transport vehicle – the Welsh 'dram' or 'tram', which held between one and two tonnes, more than twice the capacity of the 'tubs' of other British coalfields. Consequently the horses used to haul them were usually bigger than those used elsewhere in the UK.

Welsh colliery horses were usually around 15 hands high (a hand is 10cms, and horses are measured to the shoulder). However, ponies, of about 13 hands, were used for light haulage duties.

The vast majority of colliery horses were male and usually geldings, although some stallions were kept. It was claimed that the best pit horses were Welsh Cobs but, occasionally, larger horses such as Shires or imported Belgian horses were used, especially on the surface and in the main haulage roadways. However, when stocks of horses were low, they could be obtained from as far away as America or Russia. Unlike in American coal mines, little use was made of mules, but some donkeys were employed during the nineteenth century. One was killed in an explosion at Cwmnantddu Middle Sinking Pit in 1869, and another in the Morfa Colliery disaster of 1890.

A horse being brought to Point of Ayr Colliery from Mostyn Station, 1959

Legislation eventually dictated that a horse had to be at least four years old before being accepted for colliery work. This was determined by examining the teeth. A mining text book of 1893 gives the average life expectancy of a colliery horse at that time as being between eight and nine years, with around six per cent of them being killed in accidents. By the 1950s this had increased to between ten and fifteen years, although there were some who were still working on 'light jobs' at over twenty years of age.

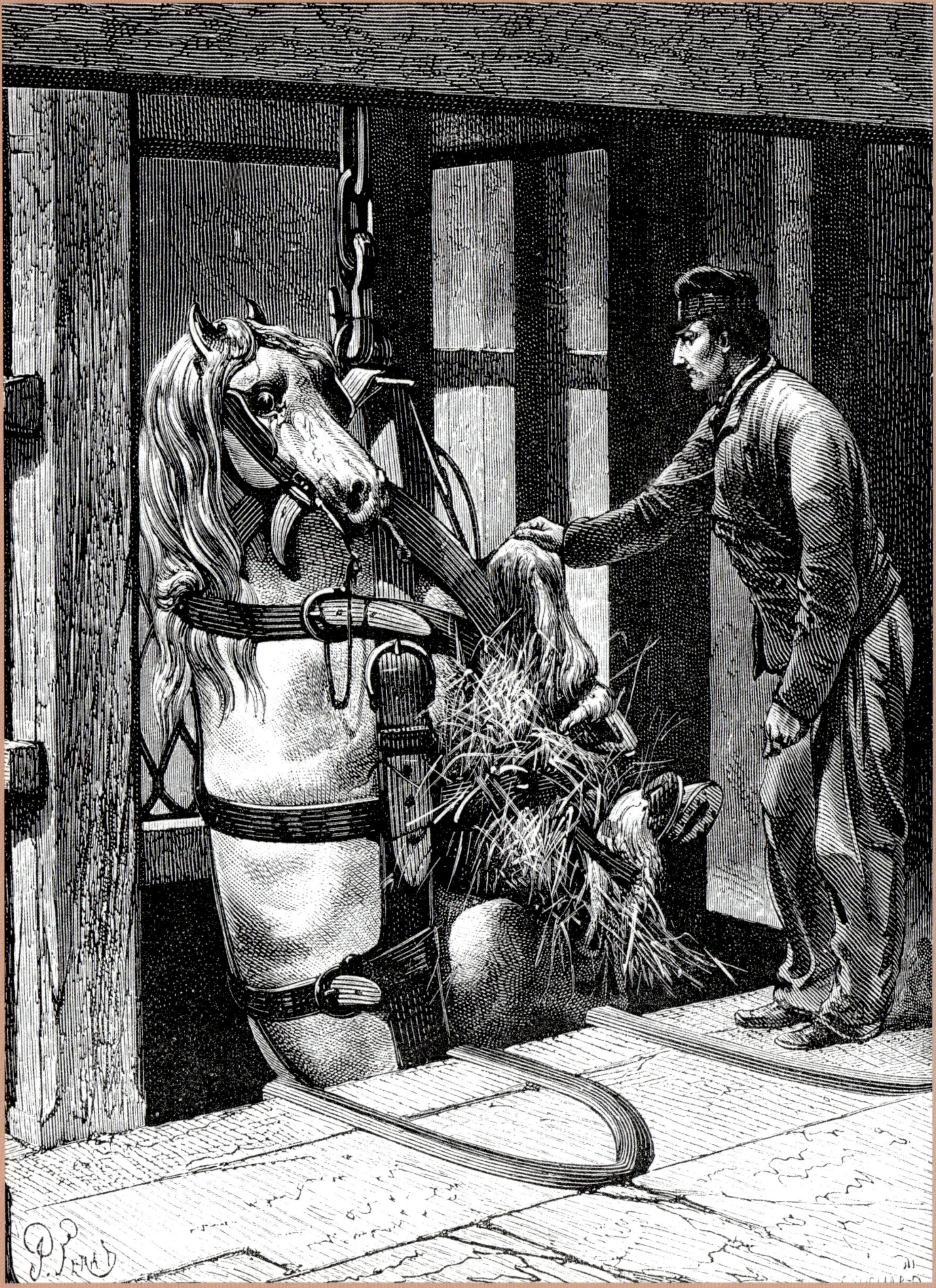

Getting them underground

Many that are taken down never see the light of day again
The Colliery Manager's Handbook, 1891

On being selected, and before being sent underground, new horses underwent a short training period. This was to see if they were suited to the work and to accustom them to the weight and feel of the harness and to the noise of a working colliery.

Horses that worked on the surface of a colliery or in a drift mine were usually stabled above ground. Horses that were chosen to work in a shaft mine were usually down there for life, unless brought up during an industrial dispute or for a horse show, until paid holidays for mineworkers were introduced in the mid-twentieth century.

Transporting horses through the shaft was a problematic and dangerous operation, both for the animals and for the men undertaking the task. When carrying horses through the shaft, the cage was converted into a type of horse box:

> To bring the horses up (or when sending them down) you'd line the inside of the cage with a kind of wooden box. It had already been made and was kept at the top of the pit. It had sides, bottom and doors so he (the horse) wouldn't hurt himself if he kicked about.
> Mel Payne, Pitman, Penallta Colliery, 1961-91

As can be imagined, a frightened animal would bite and kick out against the nearest object or person and many miners recall the sound of animals kicking the wooden sides of the cage in panic as they travelled down the shaft. Although this was a potentially dangerous procedure, the National Coal Board claimed, in their 1958 publication *Pit Ponies*, 'There is no record of even a slight accident, much less a fatality in raising or lowering horses'. However, two separate cases of horses kicking away the doors of cages and falling several hundred feet to their deaths were reported to the Secretary for Mines by the Pit Ponies' Protection Society in 1935 alone.

Left: *Descent of a horse down a mine shaft* by Louis Simonin, in *Mines and Miners*, 1869
Above: A cage fitted with wooden doors and sides for carrying horses through the shaft

A new horse learning to haul a dram at St John's Colliery, Maesteg, 1952

Pulling tubs – the north-Walian term for drams or trams – at Point of Ayr Colliery, 1959

If the cage was too small, or the horse too large, the animal could be lowered down the shaft in a net or suspended by slings. This could be a terrifying ordeal:

> Employment of slings for the lowering of ponies into the mine is worthy of condemnation. Ponies have been known to scream in terror on being lifted from the ground in slings and suspended over the open shaft.
> **R. L. Layfield, HM Horse Inspector in Mines, 1930**

Underground training

Further training occurred below ground to determine if the horse was suitable for both the physical work and the harsh underground environment. The new horse was given to a trainer-haulier, who received extra pay for the task. For a few weeks the animal was only driven along the easier, straighter roadways.

> The new pony would charge along with the empty tram rattling behind him. The animal showed fear at every stride, his eyes bulging, his back legs kicking, head tossing, and often snorting, and sometimes ending up with the empty tram off the rails and his gear in a tangle. At such times the trainer-haulier was very patient and attentive, speaking in a gentle voice and stroking the animal to quieten him. At the road head the pony was unhitched from the empty tram, turned around and backed to the full tram, and then hitched to the plate. This procedure was always

fraught with difficulty, for the new pony kicked, jumped, tossed his head and sometimes bolted.
Robert Morgan, *My lamp still burns*, 1981

Some horses never accepted their new career, and had to be sent back to the dealers who had originally supplied them.

Names

Once accepted for colliery work, the horse's coat was clipped and his mane and tail shaved to make grooming easier. He was also given an official colliery name. The following poem, translated from Welsh, gives a sample of horses' names at Point of Ayr Colliery in north Wales during the 1950s.

The Point of Ayr Ponies

Empty the stables now, the lot,
Idle the brush and ostler.
The embrocation is no more
And no-one calls the farrier.

Once we had Blackburn, Twm and Marc,
Pengwern and Cyrnol, Monty;
Tyrffi and Duke, the kicker Dic,
Once we had Sam and Batty.

Some bore a politician's name,
Bevin and Churchill, Attlee;
But also a more honest breed,
Colier and Sadler, Paddy.

The smallest one was Cherry Bach,
Then Prins, and Pwnsh and Dingo.
To boost the language of the pit,
One pony was named Cymro.

Dobbin, Llambert, and strangely, Wales,
Turpin and also Cobler,
Nelson and Bangor, Ben and Jim,
Jolly and Pinto, Trooper.

Now to the pass bye no-one turns,
The flick' ring light is banished.
The coal face drivers curse no more,
The horse shoe sound has vanished.

Einion Evans, Point of Ayr Colliery

'Twm' – one of the Point of Ayr horses featured in the poem – before going to a horse show in 1959

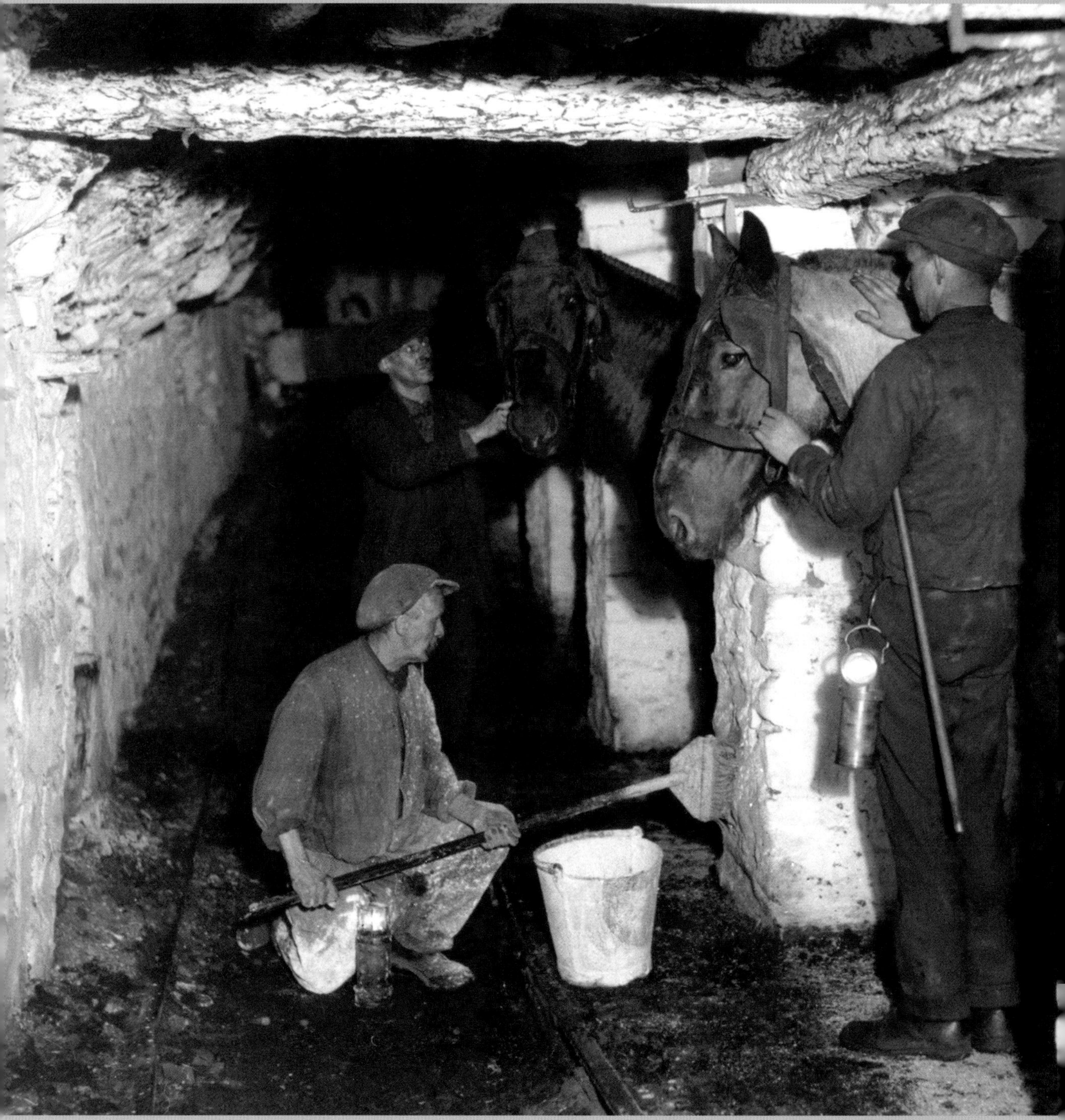

Life in the colliery

The stables

Underground stables had to be constructed very early in a colliery's life, and were therefore situated near the pit bottom. As colliery workings became more extensive, the horses spent more of their time travelling to and from their stables; to solve this problem, new stables were often constructed nearer to the working places.

The construction of underground stables varied from colliery to colliery. They were usually formed by making an opening in the gob or by widening a roadway of sufficient size to accommodate anything from fourteen to fifty horses. It was arranged for a ventilation current of clean fresh air to pass through the stables, with the used air going directly into the return airway. This avoided the smell of manure passing through the working places – an arrangement that doubtlessly pleased the colliers.

In the stables, each horse had its own stall. These were around six feet wide and twelve feet long and equipped with a manger and water bucket, although water troughs were also provided at the entrances to the stables. The stables were cleaned daily and fresh straw or sawdust placed on the floors. Behind the stalls ran a four-foot tramway to enable the manure and used sawdust to be taken out of the pit in drams; this waste was much sought after by the keen gardeners among the workforce. The stables were whitewashed on a regular basis and usually lit in some way; by the 1940s, most had electric lighting.

Rats and cats

The straw and horse feed in the stables were a magnet for rats or mice. One miner turned this to his advantage:

> Now there was a chap there, a roadman, who had a nickname – Hockey. One day we were coming up the pit and he has this sack over his back. I said 'What have you got by there Hockey?' 'Rats' he said 'for the greyhounds. I take the greyhounds out into the field and let a rat loose and they go after it and kill it; and when they go racing, after they've had a rat – Duw they go!' So I said 'How do you catch them then?' 'I catch them in the stables. You can come down tomorrow and I'll show you.' So right I go down with him now. There was a sort of container, a

Left: Underground stables, probably Penallta Colliery, about 1940
Above: A manger and stall in Western Colliery, Nantymoel, about 1972

kind of big bin, for the horses' food. He put a piece of wood from the floor up to the edge of the bin; on the bin he balanced a flat bit of board; on the edge of the board he balanced a piece of slate and on the end of the slate he put a little pile of oats to encourage the rat up – the rat would go up to the oats and fall into the bin!
Ivor Davies, Electrician, Penallta Colliery, 1958-88

A more conventional way of getting rid of rats or mice was to keep a cat in the stables. Bill Richards encountered one in 1955:

It was the first time I had been in an underground stable ... I recall that there were about twelve stalls and as I approached the last I saw a cat sitting on the rear quarters of the occupant ... It was the first time I had seen a cat underground and, observing it in what I perceived to be a cruel environment, I put out my hand to comfort it. Simultaneously I heard a warning from Joss 'Don't touch the cat mind!' Instinctively I withdrew my hand – but not quick enough. As if electrified, the cat, claws bared, slashed at me. Spitting menacingly, it moved forward on the horse's back and, fearing for my face and eyes, I retreated swiftly!
Bill Richards, Cambrian Colliery

By the 1980s only a few horses were left working underground in Wales and many of these were stabled on the surface. The last horses stabled underground in Wales were probably those at Tower Colliery, which were made redundant at the start of the 1984-5 strike.

Who looked after them?

The management of horses needed two types of specialist workers: those that supervised the animal at work and those that cared for them while 'off duty'.

In the stables, a horse-keeper was responsible for grooming, feeding and watering up to fifteen horses in his charge, as well as cleaning and repairing the tack (the harness, collar and so on). The horse-keepers would be under the supervision of the farrier (or overman horse-keeper), who would inspect the horses and stables daily to ensure that the keepers were carrying out their work satisfactorily. It was also the farrier's job to report sick horses to the veterinary surgeon, and he had the power to stop any horse being worked over the limit he thought proper.

During their working shifts, each colliery had a master haulier, who managed the assistant master hauliers, who supervised all the hauliers and horses in an underground district.

The haulier (or driver in north Wales) was responsible for the horse during its working shift. At the start of the shift he had to harness the horse, see that the collar was clean and well-fitting and make sure that the horse had its bag of feed. He had to take the horse to and from his working place and feed, water and properly manage him throughout the shift.

A horse up on the surface at National Colliery, Wattstown, November 1968

The duty of the haulier is to drive the horse and tram, or carriage, from the wall-face, where the colliers are picking the coal, to the mouth of the level. He has to look after his horse, feed him in the day, and take him home at night; his occupation requires great agility in the narrow and low-roofed roads; sometimes he is required to stop his tram suddenly – in an instant he is between the rail and the side of the level, and in almost total darkness slips a sprig (sprag) between the spokes of his tram-wheel, and is back in his place with amazing dexterity; although it must be confessed, with all his activity, he frequently gets crushed. The haulier is generally from 14 to 17 years of age, and his size is of some importance, according to the present height and width of main roads.
Report of the Children's Employment Commission, 1842

King George V meeting a young haulier (centre) and his horse at Lewis Merthyr Colliery in 1912. Below the haulier's waistcoat, you can see the leather *pishin tin*, which protected the small of his back

By the twentieth century, however, there was a wider age range among hauliers.

> There is very naturally a marked affection between a haulier and his horse. The horses, too, have their own habits and prejudices, and once a custom has been established it is rigidly adhered to as by trade union right. There are some horses too which have a nationalistic complex and appear only to respond when addressed in Welsh, a language which can be rather more vehement than English.
> **G. A. Watson, Area No2 General Manager, NCB South Western Division, 1952**

> I remember Edgar, a little haulier, who used to say to his horse every morning 'Are you going to work for me today?' Then he'd give him an apple. They were more butties (mates) than workman and horse!
> **Len Howell, Six Bells Colliery, 1960s**

The haulier was equipped with a leather belt, which threaded through a wide piece of leather positioned at the small of the back and was known in Welsh as a *pishin tin* ('arse piece'). This was designed to protect the lower spine, as hauliers carried out a great deal of lifting and pushing of loaded drams during their shift. They also carried a spare metal 'small pin', which joined the 'gun' to the shaft and could sometimes shear under the tension.

A blacksmith shoeing a horse at Lewis Merthyr Colliery, about 1910

Tack and shoes

Outside each stall they hung the tack up. The last piece that had to be hung up there was what we called the 'arse pad' – on the back of the horse's arse was a leather pad. And the reason for that was when the ostler came through the stables at the end of the shift he would look at these arse pads and if there was a scratch on one he'd say to the overman and to the haulier the following morning that so and so horse is not going out until you've repaired the height for him. It didn't matter about us being doubled up but that horse, the scratch being caused by the roof being too low, the floor had to be cut for that horse before he went out in the morning.
Vince Court, NUM Lodge Chairman, Penallta Colliery

A complete set of pit pony harness consists of: Collar and hames for draft purposes; saddle or pad, together with back-strap to carry the front end of the limbers; top-piece with bearing-strap and a belly-band to sustain the rear end of the limbers when detached from a tub or tram; breeching for backing a tub and to prevent it getting on to a pony's heels when descending a gradient; bridle and eye-guard, and, finally, the bit and reins.
***The Colliery Guardian*, 15 August 1930**

In addition, a curved metal 'limber' or 'shaft' was usually strapped around the horse during the working shift. This was attached by a 'small pin' to a dogleg length of metal known as the 'gun' which, in turn, was attached to the dram by a 'large pin'.

Some duties called for a horse to be harnessed in 'traces' rather than a 'shaft and gun'.

> I remember one horse, when he fancied a break, would lever his shoe off under a sleeper. Of course he couldn't work without a shoe and he had a rest while they sent up the pit for a replacement.
> **Len Howell, Six Bells Colliery, 1960s**

The normal method of shoeing horses is to take the horse to the blacksmith, who makes the shoe in the forge and fits it directly to the hoof, modifying it to fit. This is not possible in collieries, as underground forges would be a possible cause of fire or explosion. Instead, as each new horse was shoed before going underground, a spare set of shoes was made at the same time and kept as a template. When a horse needed a new shoe, it was made on the surface using the template and the horse was 'cold shod' underground.

What they ate

A colliery horse was fed a diet of oats supplemented with beans, maize or barley, in rations of around 6.8kg (15lbs) per day. Around 7.26kg (16lbs) of hay per horse per day was also given. In south Wales in 1931, 11,500 colliery horses consumed 58,000 tons of feed.

A horse's stomach cannot hold enough food to keep the animal going for long intervals; this meant that mangers and water troughs were usually provided along their working routes. In Wales, however, it seems to have been more usual for the horses to carry nose bags of chaff around their necks during the working shift.

Horses working above ground were sometimes fed in their stables. One in particular liked his food on time:

> There was a surface horse called Ponty – you had to make sure he was detached from the dram when the grub time hooter went at half past ten or he would drag his load across the yard back to the stables!
> **Len Howell, Six Bells Colliery, 1960s**

A haulier and pony sharing 'grub time', in the 1950s

The horses sometimes fancied a change of diet – and made sure that they got it:

> The one was called Sultan ... He was a bugger! You'd walk past him ... and if you didn't give him whatever you had left – sandwiches or whatever – he'd lash out and you'd be tight against the rings trying to get past him! ... He was a show horse with the Coal Board – the Blackwood Show and all – he won a lot.
> **Keith Williams, Deputy, Penallta Colliery**

> They would have your food if you put it down and didn't take care of it. O yeah, they'd have your food all right!
> **George Heard, Penallta Colliery, 1944-5**

And they wouldn't only cadge food:

> Another thing that the horses used to do is want a drink. They'd hang their tongues out and that was it. They could get into people's pockets, get the bottle out and drink it all! You'd very often find your bottle with its neck all squashed. It was a tin bottle, of course – glass bottles aren't allowed underground.
> **Point of Ayr Colliery miner, born 1890**

Not everything they ate was healthy:

> Even the horses used to chew tobacco! They loved tobacco, and they knew who would give them some too.
> **Point of Ayr Colliery Miner, born 1890**

And they had to get rid of it all afterwards:

> My grandfather, Albert George Powell (more popularly known as 'Quoitmer Dorsey'!) was working as a haulier at Marine Colliery. At work one day he was standing at the rear of his horse with his back to it when it picked up its tail and excreted a deluge of watery manure all over him. After the shift he had to walk home caked in dung and my grandmother made him take all his clothes off in the backyard, cursing him as she had to clean them for work the next day.
> **Andrew Williams, Electrician, Marine Colliery**

The 'Chaff Strike'

The hauliers in one Welsh colliery in 1955 stopped work because they thought that their seventeen horses weren't getting enough oats in their chaff mixture. One of the strikers reported that the horses seemed 'out of condition' as a result. It seems that the horses were fed from a common trough and some were taking the shares of the others. The strike ended when it was agreed that each horse would get his own ration of food separately.

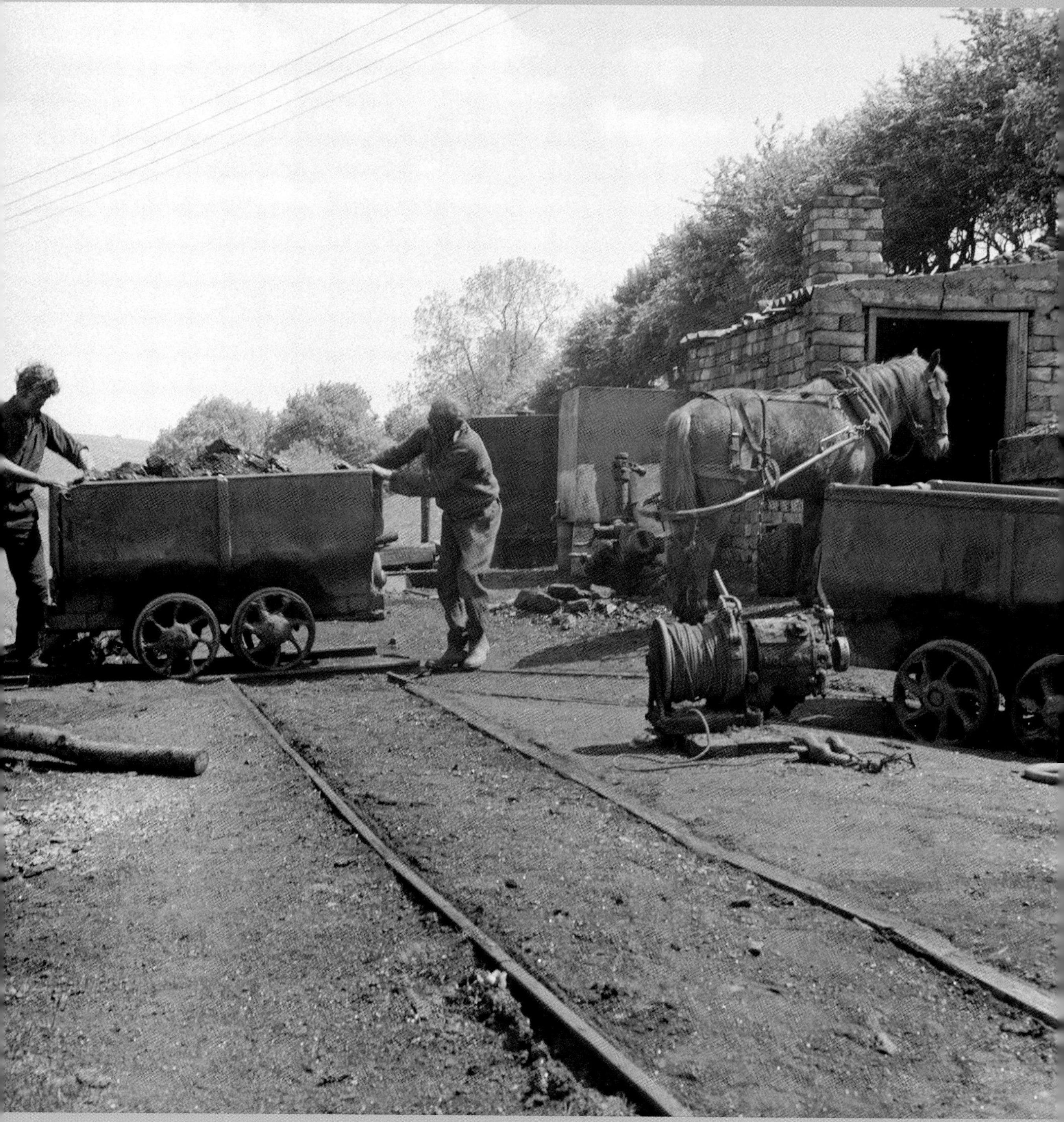

Work

From the early days of the industry, horses and ponies were used for hauling coal from the pits to the customer and, before the introduction of steam winding in the 1790s, horse-gins were very common for winding coal from underground.

The first records of ponies being used for underground haulage appear in the north of England around 1750. However, horses were only employed on a large scale after the 1842 Mines Act, which effectively abolished the underground employment of boys under the age of ten and all females. As these had provided much of the haulage in mines, they had to be replaced, and the horse was the obvious choice.

Until they were replaced by mechanical haulage, most colliery horses were employed in the movement of sledges or, later, wheeled drams of coal, from the coalface to the shaft or mine entrance.

Once a dram had been filled with coal by the colliers it was replaced by an empty one. As there was only one set of rails leading to the 'stall' (working place) this was a complicated procedure.

> The tram was scotched by placing wooden wedges underneath the rear wheels to prevent it running back when the pony was unhitched. The next event surprised me, for at a command from the haulier the pony pointed his head to the floor and turned his body through one hundred and eighty degrees. The 'tumble up' was the only place in the road wide enough for the pony to perform this manoeuvre. The 'tumble up' was a space cut into the side of the road into which the empty tram was tumbled so that the pony could pass with the full tram hitched behind him. Tumbling the empty tram into the 'tumble up' not only required much strength, but knack as well. This was performed by two men, or a man and a boy, one at either end of the tram. The inner wheels were scotched and the tram tumbled into the space. The pony was then able to leave the stall-road with his full tram of coal. The haulier would either walk in front of the pony or ride, in a crouching position, on the hitching plate. When the haulier had left the road the empty tram was tumbled back on the rails and pushed to the road-head where it was secured with scotches and sprags.
> Robert Morgan, *My lamp still burns*, 1981

Left: A horse and dram at Ffynonau Duon Colliery, 1974
Above: *Horse powered winding gin* by Paul Sandby, about 1778

The horse, attached to his heavy load, then had to negotiate the difficult colliery roadways.

> As to the work performed by horses, much depends upon circumstances. On a favourable road having a slight descent for the full tubs a 14-hand pony may be able to draw 10 tons at a time ... where a horse works up a steep road, a considerable jerk and strain are necessary to start the load, especially if the back wheels near the (coal) face are beyond the rails and rest on a miry or uneven floor. Such strains are very injurious to the animals...
>
> ...The useful performance of a horse underground is to convey about 45 tons one mile per day. Some horses travel from twenty to twenty-five miles in a shift underground, others do not exceed six. The heavier the gradient and more irregular the roadway, the less will be the distance travelled.
> **The Colliery Manager's Handbook, 1891**

Commands

Colliery horses were trained to respond to verbal commands. Common ones were:

Gun on (or See-way) – turn right
Come here – turn left
Come here back – turn around
Come back – walk backwards

A plain representation of the teams and trams of coal brought down to Pwllgwenlly by John Thomas, 1821

Many horses would only respond when spoken to in Welsh. During the 1904-5 Religious Revival, it was said that, because many hauliers had given up swearing at them, the horses got confused!

The working day

The working hours for both colliery horses and miners have varied over the years – in the 1840s they could be very long indeed.

> I go out with the horse about six or seven o'clock in the morning, and work almost 12 hours every day. There are no regular times to stop; I often eat my bread and cheese on the tram going in and out; the horse has a 'nose-bag'.
> **Rees Jones, Haulier, aged 13,**
> **Report of the Children's Employment Commission, 1842**

By the 1930s, most horses worked between forty-five and sixty hours a week. In 1949 their maximum working hours were laid down as being not more than forty-eight hours per week and no more than seven shifts per week. They were also entitled to the same twenty minute 'grub break' as the men.

> I had never handled a horse before but one of the hauliers asked me to take a horse and dram of coal out of the small drift mine I was working in. Horses always seemed to know when it was the last dram of the day and this one shot off like a rocket towards the drift entrance and daylight. I didn't have enough sense to let go of the rope and shot off with it. My

legs were flicking up in the air like a circus clown but I still kept hold –
I could see us both hurtling over the coal chute at the drift mouth and I
thought I was a goner! Fortunately the horse knew exactly where to stop
and did so very sharply. I never offered to take a horse out again!
Tony Barlow, Graig y Llyn Mine, Rhigos

At the end of a hard day the horses were washed and groomed to get rid of the coal dust before being stabled:

At Glyntillery, around 1973, we had two horses which were stabled on
the surface and taken down the drift every morning to work
underground. At the end of the shift they were brought back out
stinking dirty and were hosed down with freezing cold water from a
mountain stream. It always amazed me how they just stood there, they
never used to move or complain – they were hard, tough old buggers!
Paul Meredith, Glyntillery Drift Mine

Left: Tony Barlow and a horse at Graig y Llyn Mine, Rhigos, 1993
Right, top: A horse with a loaded (or 'raced') dram at Ferndale
Right, bottom: Underground at Darran Colliery, Neath Abbey, about 1974

35

Ceffyle Pwll y Bigyn! ('Bigyn Pit Horses!')

Saith neu wyth o geffyle glew,
Dim ond esgyrn, croen a blew!
Ceffyle Pwll y Bigyn,
Ceffyle Pwll y Bigyn,
Ceffyle Pwll y Bigyn,
Dim ond esgyrn, croen a blew!

('Seven or eight brave horses,
Only bones, skin and hair!
Bigyn pit horses,
Bigyn pit horses,
Bigyn pit horses,
Nothing but bones, skin and hair!')

Bigyn Colliery, which had worked through most of the nineteenth century, closed in 1893. My grandfather (b.1888) had recited this little poem/song to my father who passed it on to me. The words paint a jaundiced view of the appearance of the horses in at least one late nineteenth-century colliery.
Robert Protheroe Jones, Curator of Heavy Industry, Amgueddfa Cymru – National Museum Wales

Cruelty in 'secret places'?

> In these secret places are employed many human beings, horses, ponies and donkeys; and it may be reasonably assumed, without proof even, that the thick darkness that prevails therein shrouds many acts of cruelty.
> *The Animal World*, January 1878

There has been much dispute over the years as to how horses really were treated underground.

> Placed in the hands of ignorant lads who shamefully abused the powers entrusted to them without fear of punishment, worked often in double shifts of sixteen consecutive hours, kept below ground for years without seeing daylight, left without any form of inspection worthy of the name, their lives were a standing outcry against cruelty and injustice.
> *The Animal World*, September 1918

> Many unkind things have been said and are continuing to be repeated by persons who know nothing of underground conditions, and whose ignorance leads them to make statements for public consumption which are very wide of the mark, and are wholly mischievous.
>
> The colliery horse is neither badly treated, badly housed, nor badly fed. Those in whose care horses are placed are, like their critics and the rest of us, fallible, but for the very great majority I will say at once that they are skilled and humane in their treatment and care of the horses.
>
> Horses cost a lot of money and, apart altogether from the necessity upon humane grounds for kindness, skilful care and treatment will enhance their value and give a better return upon capital expended upon them.
> **Inspector of Mines, Cardiff and Forest of Dean Division, 1929**

B. L. Coombes, a collier who related many details of his working life underground during the first half of the twentieth century, had his own view of how horses were treated.

Left: A haulier bringing out coal in the early 1900s

The Pit Pony Protection Society

This society was founded by David Jeffrey Williams (1888-1972) in 1927 and he remained its secretary for forty-one years. The society was totally against the use of horses and ponies in mines and fought a bitter propaganda battle with the coal owners; they certainly annoyed the West Yorkshire Coal Owners Association, which described the society's membership in 1927 as 'composed of a company of old ladies of both sexes'.

Among their aims were the increased mechanization of mine haulage, which would lessen the need for horses underground, and the adoption of electric 'cap lamps' on horses' head harnesses. They advertised in, and wrote letters to, the press, they lobbied parliament and encouraged both public and private bodies to buy coal from collieries that didn't use horses. They were especially critical of the display of colliery horses in agricultural shows, which they regarded as propaganda. By 1967 they were still active and applauding the adoption of new energy sources to replace the coal industry – 'The ponies in our mines have two new allies, namely nuclear power and North Sea gas … The ponies as a result may disappear from the pits even before 1970'.

However, by the late 1960s, the society was in decline. It was taken over as a separate unit within the RSPCA for a short time, before being finally wound up during the 1970s.

21,240 PONIES STILL USED IN MINES —

21,240 too many!

Reid Report (1945) condemned pony-haulage in mines as out of date.

Please help the
Pit Ponies' Protection Society
69, Carlton Hill, London, N.W.8

FAIR PLAY FOR -
PIT PONIES

After two years of continuous employment underground, ponies should have one month's rest on the surface in Homes of Rest owned and maintained by the National Coal Board.

All horses and ponies to have their collars fitted with electric battery lamps, or, alternatively, that their haulage roads be provided with electric light.

Within a reasonable time all mines should have pony-haulage roads large enough in every way to allow ponies of not less than 14 hands high to be employed.

An adequate fully-trained reserve of ponies to be kept above ground in suitable places approved by H.M. Inspectors of Horses in Mines at larger collieries or group of collieries for use in cases of emergency or need or for rota service when bringing ponies to the surface for rest or for compassionate reasons.

Only one shift to be worked by ponies in every 24 hours, and reports in writing to be sent to the Divisional Inspector of any emergency calling for the working of longer hours.

Over-loading of ponies to be prevented.

Loose boxes, not stalls, to be provided in all underground stables.

Veterinary surgeons to be employed by the Ministry of Power, not by the National Coal Board, to examine ponies every six months as to their fitness to continue to work below ground.

Homes of Rest for retired ponies to be provided by the National Coal Board, and the N.C.B. also to maintain discarded unfit ponies sent to other Homes of Rest.

THE PIT PONIES' PROTECTION SOCIETY
120. LOUDOUN ROAD, LONDON, N.W.8.

Advertisements by the Pit Pony Protection Society in 1947 (above) and 1967 (right)

> I have read statements in which it is argued that there is no cruelty to horses underground ... These writers may believe what they write, but I do not ... It is in the actual working that cruelty occurs ... I have seen a horse that was blind in one eye rubbing its nose against the sharp stones so that it could feel the way to turn, and being whipped for not coming round fast enough ... Every day horses are worked for sixteen and more hours straight off ... very often they have no water at all during those long hours in the hot places of the mine ... I have seen horses drop from exhaustion several times during a shift ... Often a man must choose between forcing an exhausted horse and being sent home on the dole ... he must choose whether the horse shall suffer, or his wife and children.

Coombes also tells of horses being driven through low headings, forcing them to rip their backs on the stones of the roof:

> ...the horse, with stones ripping into his back and his mouth twisted by the chain that stops him rushing away from this torture, does the thing that his instinct tells him is the only way to get free – and kicks. After that first kick he is marked as a dangerous horse ... and is treated as such.
> **B. L. Coombes, *These poor hands*, 1939**

There is little doubt that the pressure on both management and workers to get the coal out as quickly as possible could lead to cruelty. This was especially true in an industry where the handling of horses was mainly the responsibility of men and boys who hadn't come from an agricultural background. The truth probably lies somewhere between the two extremes:

> You hear about cruelty to horses underground. The thing is that if someone beat a horse it would get stubborn and not want to work. It would also bide its time and wait for when it could get him between itself and the side of the roadway so that it could crush him against the side. Horses are not dull and, if they are treated with respect, they will do anything for you. They were often spoilt – we used to bring the vegetable peelings from the house for them.
> **Tony Barlow, Graig y Llyn Mine, Rhigos**

The treatment of horses appears to have improved during the twentieth century, due to both legislation and the adoption of mechanical conveying, which meant that they were less relied on for the transport of coal.

Legislation

Until the 1880s the welfare of colliery horses and ponies was left to chance. The first legislation to protect them was part of the Coal Mines Regulations Act of 1887. The Act allowed mine inspectors to investigate how horses were treated and whether there was enough height in mine roadways to allow them to travel through safely. However, these regulations were too limited to prevent the injuries and neglect that still occurred. This is an extract from a pamphlet entitled *Don'ts for Miners and Mine Officials* produced by the *Western Mail* in 1899:

> Don't ill treat the horse for every little mishap, especially when it arises from your carelessness.
>
> Don't throw stones or sprags at horses.
>
> Don't place your food box in the horse's nose bag.
>
> Don't assume a horse works better on an empty nose bag.

In 1911, major protective legislation followed protests by groups such as the National Equine Defence League. This was the most important Act passed for the protection of horses employed in mines. The third schedule of this Act was modified into the 1949 and 1956 Acts, which became known as The Pit Ponies' Charter.

The Pit Ponies' Charter

> No horse shall go underground until it is four years old and certified free from glanders.
>
> Every horse shall be examined once at least in every twelve months by a veterinary surgeon.
>
> Any horse certified as permanently unfit for work or work in the mine shall as soon as practicable be brought to the surface.
>
> Any horse unfit for work shall be destroyed immediately unless disposed of to a home of rest or to a responsible person, other than a horse dealer.
>
> Each horse shall be housed in a stall adequate in size, and supplied with clean straw or other suitable bedding.
>
> All stables shall be cleaned daily and kept in a sanitary condition; all roofs, walls and partitions not painted or made of slate, tiles, glazed brick or iron shall be lime washed once at least in every three months.
>
> Stables shall be separated from the main roads, adequately lit, ventilated with intake air, fitted with a loose box to every 25 horses, fitted with one or more drinking troughs, and floored with paving or concrete.
>
> Every loose box and stall shall be suitably drained.
>
> There shall be only one horse to a stall. Each stall shall have a manger.
>
> There shall be at least one horse-keeper to every 15 horses in the stables.

The use of blind horses was prohibited. However, it is probable that some horses became gradually blind from old age or working in poor light. Eye injuries were also common until effective protective headgear with eye guards was made compulsory in the early twentieth century.

Colliery horses and ponies were routinely checked over by Her Majesty's Inspectors of Mines. In addition, by 1913 there were eight full-time Horse Inspectors. After this year the numbers of horses employed gradually declined, but inspecting them was still a huge task. In 1956 Horse Inspectors paid 2,453 visits to mines and made 31,204 examinations of individual horses.

It should be noted that even in the late twentieth century, after decades of inspection and legislation, a few miners have confessed to the author, 'off the record', that it was normal practice to push a piece of coal into a 'lazy' horse's anus, sometimes with the help of a blow from a piece of timber, to get the animal to work.

PIT PONIES AND COLLIERY HORSES

The Facts

A Joint Reply to the pamphlet called "The Truth about Pit Ponies and Colliery Horses," issued by Mr. Philip Gee with the authority of the Coal Owners (*The Mining Association of Great Britain*), June, 1933.

Published by
THE R.S.P.C.A., 105 Jermyn St., London, S.W.1,
THE SCOTTISH S.P.C.A., 19 Melville St., Edinburgh 3,
and
THE PIT PONIES' PROTECTION SOCIETY,
82 Boundary Road, London, N.W.8.

LEAFLET B.   See Leaflet A for Examples of Cases of Cruelty.

THE SUFFERINGS OF PIT PONIES

A VICTIM OF THE MINES.
One of the Ponies in R.S.P.C.A.
Conviction Case No. A8737

Remember Horses are kept for years in tomblike darkness underground that you may have comfort.

ISSUED BY THE
ROYAL SOCIETY FOR THE PREVENTION OF CRUELTY TO ANIMALS
105, JERMYN STREET, LONDON, S.W.1.

Catastrophe de Courrières
Cadavre de Cheval

Danger, injuries and death

Horse sense

An animal's instincts could be invaluable in detecting any unfamiliar conditions or atmosphere underground:

> A horse was in as much danger underground as a man. And a horse could sense danger before a man could. Say a horse was standing here at a heading, and he heard something working above him, it would squeal like a baby. It would give a sign, telling you 'Look, move me out of here quick! Something is going to come down here now!' The creature had that sense.
> **Cwmavon Miner, born 1900**

> I don't know if they were all like this but in our pit the horses wouldn't let you walk in front of them. They used to butt you out of the way – they would even bite you at times if you weren't out of their way quick enough. The reason seemed to be that they liked to know what was in front of them, what dangers there might be, and if you blocked their view – God help you!
> **Tony Barlow, Graig y Llyn Mine, Rhigos**

Accidents and illness

In spite of this 'sixth sense', many horses were killed or injured at work.

> Horses receive injury from falling in the workings, or running away and wedging themselves into roads too low for them, and many are injured or killed by falls of roof, run-away drams, explosions, etc.
> ***The Colliery Manager's Handbook*, 1891**

In 1914 the RSPCA reported that out of 70,396 animals employed in British coal mines, 2,999 suffered injuries resulting in death, while 10,878 had received non-fatal injuries. These figures did not include horses destroyed because of old age.

Left: A horse killed in an explosion at Courrieres Colliery in France, 1906. The legs were removed in order to fit the body onto the trolley

Day-to-day injuries included injuries to the legs and hooves from the uneven surfaces underground, 'roofing' or scraping the back in low roadways, and head and eye injuries – although these were less of a problem when head and eye protection was made compulsory in 1911. Horses could also get caught up in wire haulage ropes, which could cause serious friction burns, cuts and puncture wounds. They could also be crushed against ventilation doors or the sides of roadways.

Two drams had come off the rails, knocked out a few timber supports and the side coal had come out pinning the horse which had been pulling the drams against the side of the roadway. He was cut very badly and his ribs were probably smashed – he was squealing with pain – an awful noise that I will never forget, it was heartbreaking. I was told to run and get a shot firing battery, a length of shot wire and a detonator. The detonator was pushed into the horse's ear and fired killing the horse instantly. I don't think that was at all legal but you couldn't let a horse suffer like that. I think that everyone involved was in tears.
Interview with former miner who wished to remain anonymous

…near Bridgend 40 horses suffering from a bad form of grease … Near Tondu several horses were found at one place with bad lacerations on their backs, caused by contact with jagged roofs, at another pit 30 horses … nearly all very lame … Near Bargoed 27 horses were found whose heads, withers and backs were lacerated by cuttings described as very low and jagged.
***The Animal World*, January 1878**

All horses are prone to particular illnesses and ailments but conditions underground tended to make some much worse. Very wet conditions underfoot caused 'grease heel', an unpleasant condition that left the lower legs raw, swollen and oozing with pus. Horses also suffered the same dust-related illnesses as the miners, leaving many horses 'broken winded'. To illustrate this, Cyfarthfa Castle Museum has a solid ball of stone dust, weighing over a pound, which was taken from a colliery horse's lung that had died of silicosis.

The dim light underground also contributed to the development of cataracts which, untreated, could lead to blindness. There is a popular belief among the public that all colliery horses go blind, but a blind horse would not have been very productive, and it is doubtful that the management would have tolerated an animal that did not pay its way. Whatever the truth, it has been illegal to have a blind horse working underground since 1911.

Left, top: A ball of stone dust removed from a dead colliery horse's lung *(Courtesy of Cyfarthfa Castle Museum & Art Gallery, Merthyr Tydfil)*
Left, bottom: A horse being treated at Tondu Horse Hospital, 1953

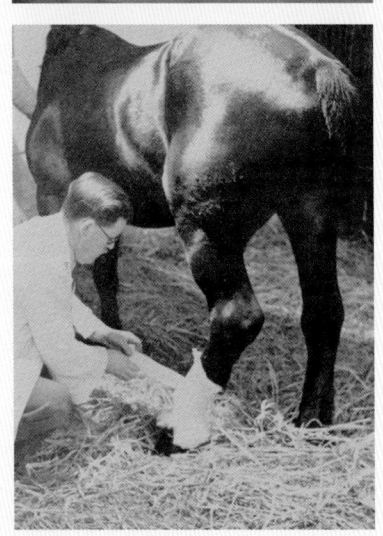

A horse on the surface with Evan Jones, the driver (left), and Mr Cartwright, the colliery vet, at Point of Ayr Colliery, 1959

Sick or injured horses were either treated underground in the special stalls provided in the stables or taken to the surface if they were likely to be ill for some time.

In 1947 the first, and probably only, hospital for sick or injured colliery horses in Britain was set up at Tondu House near Bridgend in south Wales. The hospital could accommodate up to twenty horses and included a dispensary, isolation stalls and an operating stall specially fitted for the administration of local anaesthetics. Each stall had a water tap that could be turned on by pressure from the horse's muzzle. Convalescent horses were turned out into fields surrounding the stables.

Disasters

> The fumes coming from the (main) Stables was awful, that place was like a furnace we could see the poor animals blazing up and bursting like crackers...
>
> ...we went into the little stable there were I think six horses there chard to a sinder and a cat sat on the hip of a horse chard like a coke and stuck fast like if it was melted there.
> **William (surname unknown), describing the recovery of Cambrian Colliery following the 1905 disaster.** *(Courtesy of Bill Richards, 2006)*

A cartoon from *Coal News*, about 1950

The Risca Colliery explosion of 1880 killed all sixty-nine underground horses as well as 120 men. In 1894 an exploratory party of fifty-two men was sent down the Albion Colliery to find a way of disposing of the 118 horses that had been killed during an explosion that had caused the deaths of 290 men and boys. During the Morfa Colliery disaster of 1890 twenty horses were known to have survived the blast in the stables. Although some of the miners begged to be allowed to attempt to rescue them, the management refused to put more human lives at risk. The poor animals eventually died of starvation, tied firmly into their stalls.

It was apparently common practice to secure the horses so that they wouldn't interfere with the evacuation of a colliery during a disaster. However, during the flooding of Caradog Vale Colliery in 1906, a horse that had been left behind survived while the men who had tethered him all drowned.

A loose, frightened horse could be very dangerous. During the Maerdy Colliery disaster of December 1885, a miner, who had survived the blast with only slight injuries, made his way to the underground stables. In the darkness he found a water trough where he could quench his thirst. As he took a drink from the trough, a horse, mad with pain and fright, rushed in from the roadway, collided with him and dropped dead, pinning him against the trough. The miner received worse injuries from the horse than from the explosion itself!

A happier story was reported by the RSPCA in 1907. During the flooding of an unnamed pit near Gorseinon, miners escaping from the inrushing water left food for a trapped horse in case a rescue attempt could later be made to save him. It apparently took seventeen days before the waters had subsided and an exploratory party could be sent down. Amazingly, the horse was 'not only alive but manifesting the keenest satisfaction at the sight once more of human beings'.

Horses injuring miners

On the other hand, colliery horses could sometimes be responsible for injuring their human workmates. The Great Western Collieries Register of Ordinary Accidents 1912 to 1917 includes seventy accidents caused directly by colliery horses. These include men being kicked, knocked down, stepped on and crushed against the side of the roadways. There are also cases of horses kicking up stones into hauliers' faces but, strangely, only one incident of biting. Although working with horses could be hazardous, it should be noted that there were over 3,000 accidents recorded in the register that were not directly caused by them.

The Great Western register only recorded non-fatal accidents, but horses could be responsible for the deaths of mine workers:

> January 28th 1905, Herbert Snook, 20 years old, Haulier. A horse bolted in a stall road and knocked him down, fracturing the base of his skull. The horse was of a nervous temperament and had apparently been frightened.
>
> August 1st 1905, Thomas David, 44 years old, Ostler, Dinas Main Colliery. Run over by tram owing to horse taking fright while taking two trams loaded with horse food along the main level.
>
> September 18th 1904, William Goddard, 48 years old, Ostler, Waun Llwyd Colliery. A horse which he was feeding rubbed against his leg, slightly scratching it. Blood poisoning set in, and he died on 3rd March 1905.
> **HM Inspectors of Mines, Annual Report, 1905**

Retirement and rest

Originally, when horses became too old or ill to work, they would usually be sent to the knackers' yard to be humanely destroyed. The meat was then used in dog food and the bones used to make glue. After the 1956 Regulations, however, it became normal to send former pit horses to one of several rest homes maintained for the purpose.

> When a horse comes to the end of its working life it is sometimes possible to place him in a reputable rest home or with an animal lover. Should an old pony be sold, there is the risk that he might fall into the hands of an unscrupulous dealer, so, if no home can be found for him, he is humanely destroyed under the supervision of a Coal Board official.
> *Pit Ponies*, **NCB publication, 1958**

Never mind the men – what about the horses?

> **A dead pony is £20 loss: A dead collier costs nothing except heartache to those left behind.**
> **Keir Hardie MP, 1910**

There was always a suspicion among the colliers that the management worried more about the health of their horses than their human workforce. However accurate this was is debateable, but the first thought of Jabez Thomas, the manager of Cymmer Old Colliery in 1856, on finding out that an explosion had occurred underground, was to ask the brakesman at the top of the shaft 'How many horses are down?' rather than enquiring about the fate of his human workforce. In the event, 114 men and boys lost their lives and forty-one were injured.

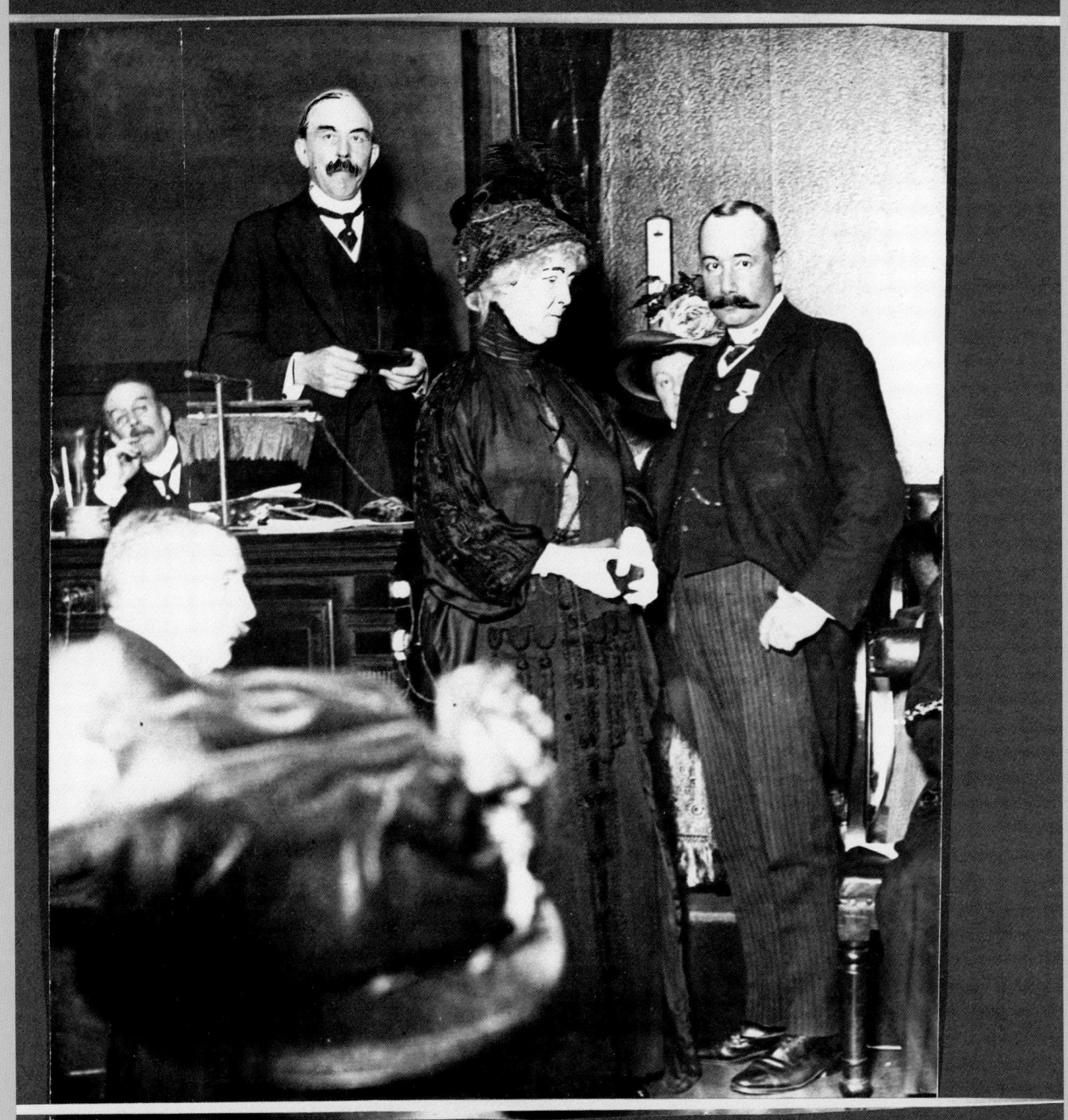

Countess of Bective presented a number of medals

Pit horses and politics

> Perhaps no action of the strikers will arouse greater indignation than their attempt to condemn the pit horses to death underground.
> *Morning Post*, 11 November 1910

In November 1910 colliery horses became part of the propaganda war between the colliery owners and strikers during the Cambrian Combine Dispute (the 'Tonypandy Riots'). Three hundred horses had been left underground at the Glamorgan Colliery and it was claimed that they had not been fed or watered for several days. In addition they were under threat of drowning, as the heavy picketing by strikers had reduced the operation of the colliery pumping system which normally kept the workings from flooding.

The press attacked the strikers for ignoring the plight of the horses, which led to a loss of sympathy from the general public. Even King George V was worried enough to ask about the matter. On the other hand, the strikers complained about the attitude of people who worried about animals when their families were suffering. In addition, they claimed that the horses could have been brought up just before or during the first week of the strike and had in fact sent a telegram to Winston Churchill, the Home Secretary, requesting that they be allowed to feed and bring up the horses.

Whatever the truth of the matter, some days later, members of the management descended the shaft and reported the horses alive and in good condition. For this action F. D. Llewelyn, agent for the Naval Colliery, was later awarded medals from both the RSPCA and Our Dumb Friends League. By the end of November the horses had all been brought to the surface.

A cavalry charge of the Class War!

During the 1874 general election campaign a large horseback procession was organized by the local Conservative party in the Rhondda. Not to be outdone, miners from Pentre Colliery got fifty horses from their colliery and staged a counter demonstration. The two groups clashed near the Cardiff Arms Hotel in Treorchy and, after a violent melee, the Tories fled back down the valley, some being thrown into the river and others injured. Around thirty people were arrested, thirteen of them being sent to jail.

Left: The Countess of Bective presenting an RSPCA medal to F. D. Llewelyn, Colliery Agent, Naval Colliery in 1911
Above: The medals presented to F. D. Llewelyn
Overleaf: Miners and horses from National Colliery, Wattstown, about 1910

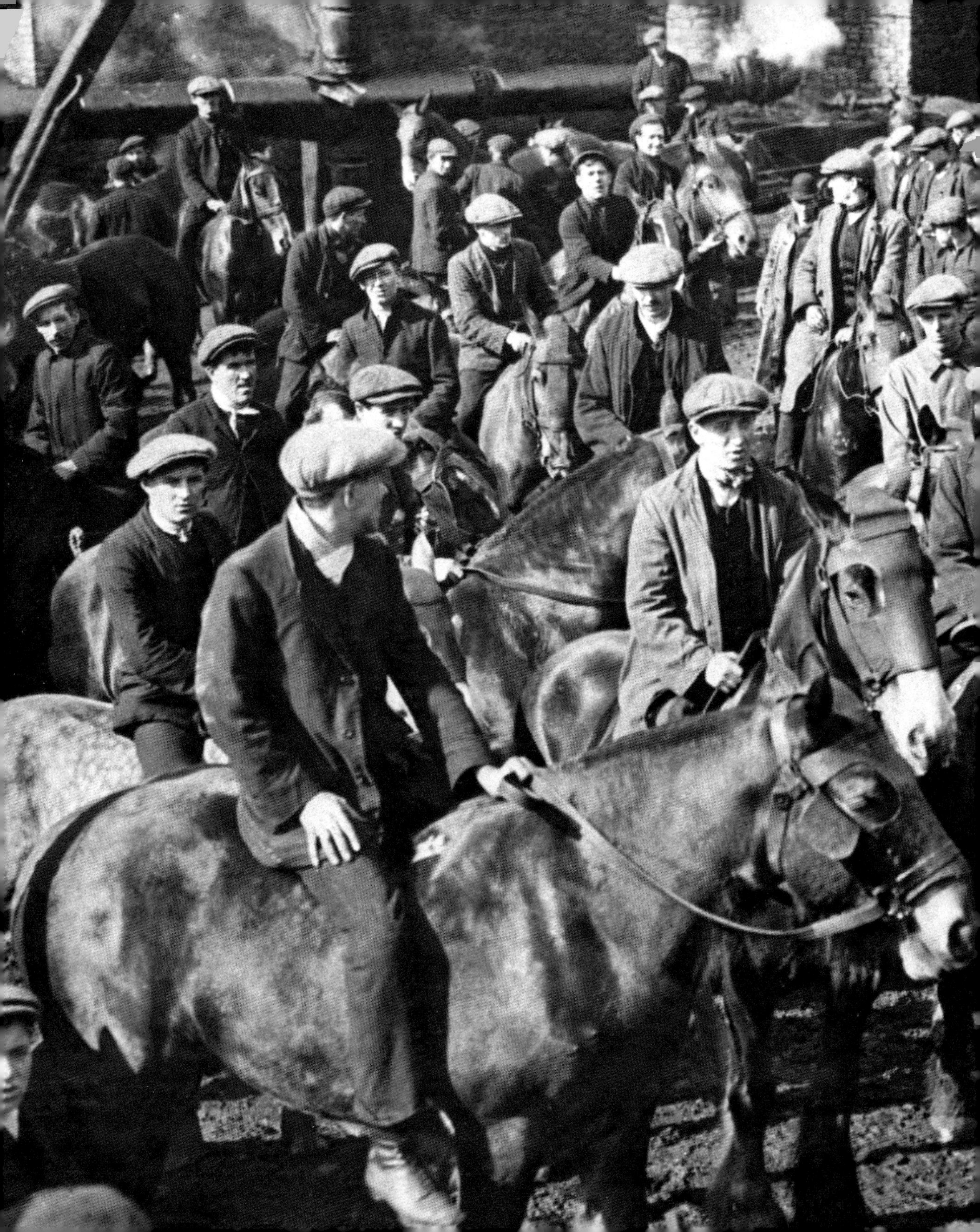

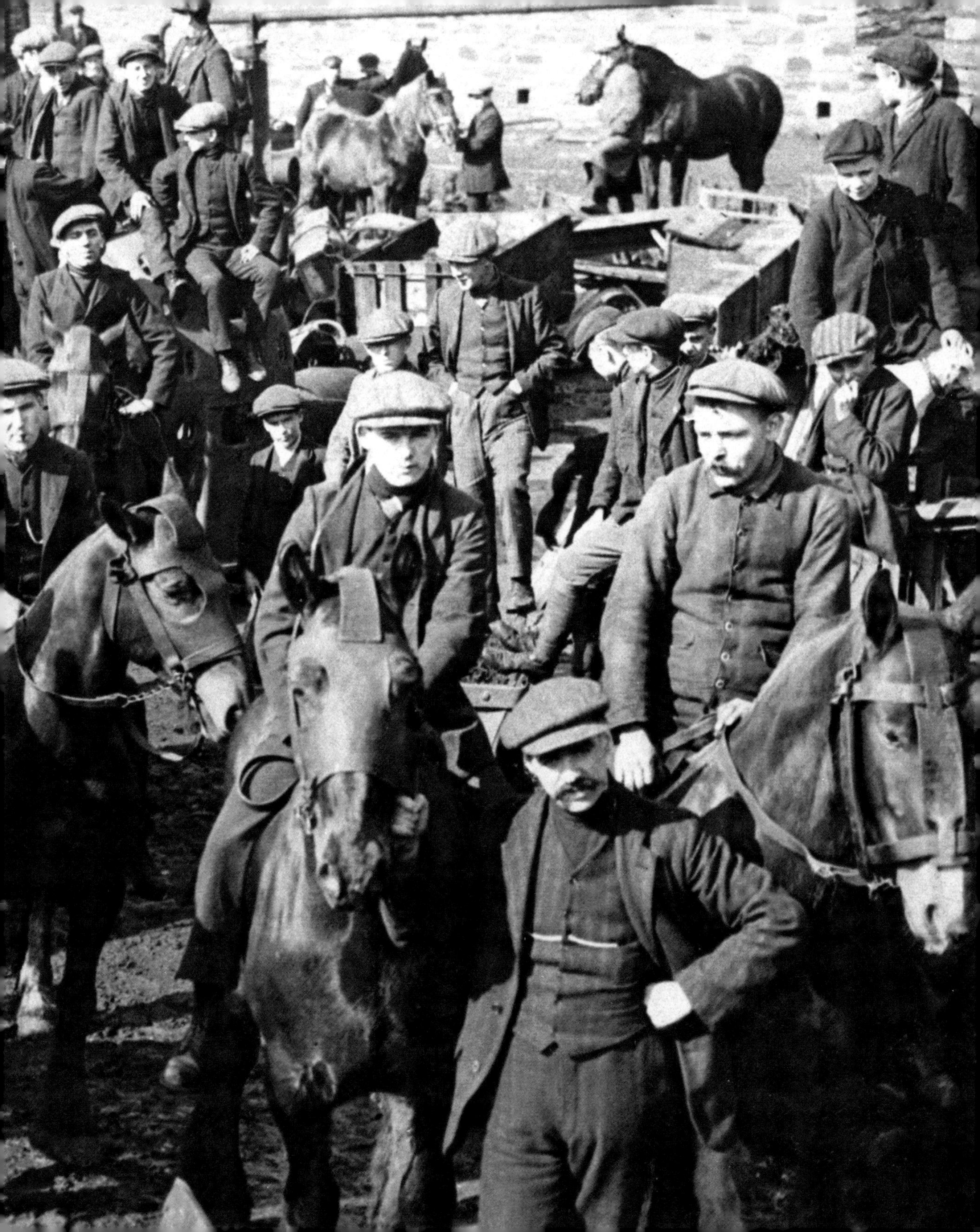

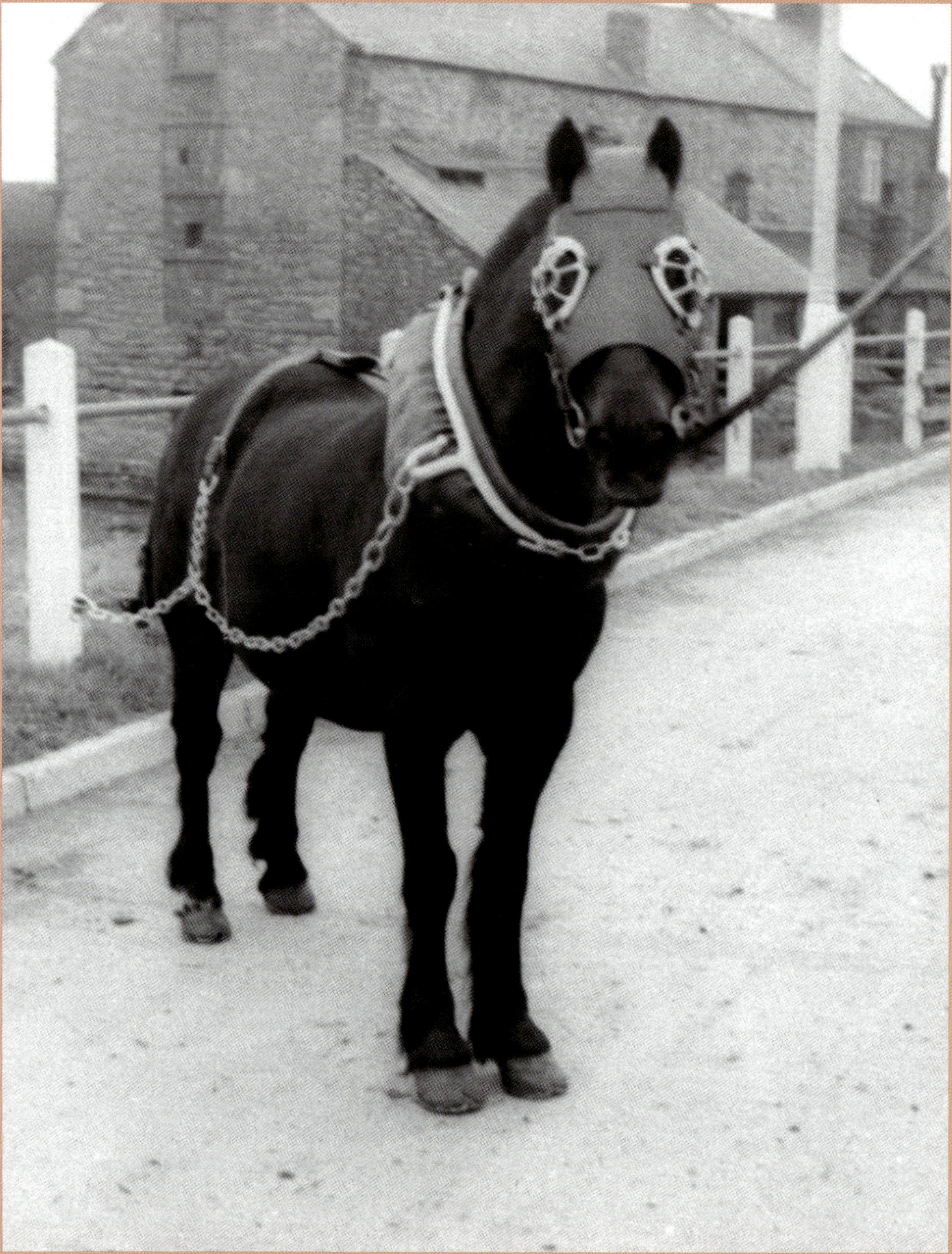

High days and holidays

> Tortured by longing for the daylight he has lost.
> *Germinal*, Emile Zola, 1885

In 1938 colliers were granted an annual week's paid holiday, and the horses were usually allowed a week above ground as well. Ten years later the colliers were given two weeks paid leave, so the horses too had an extra week.

We have seen how difficult it was to get horses down the shaft; bringing them back again needed the same procedures and was just as problematic.

Left: A horse on the surface at Point of Ayr Colliery, 1959
Above: Bringing horses up at Glyncorrwg Colliery, November 1969

A group of colliery horses at a local show in the 1930s

> The cage would be lined with timber planks and fitted with wooden doors. You could see that they were a bit apprehensive on pit bottom waiting to go into the cage – but once they were travelling up the shaft they seemed to smell the fresh air above them and started to get agitated, kicking the wooden sides sometimes. When they got out on top they were put into horse boxes and taken to the lakes in Cwmtillery where they were released into the fields. Then they knew they were free – running, kicking and jumping – just like excited kids on holiday!!
> **Len Howell, Six Bells Colliery, 1960s**

The horses' first instinct was to establish a pecking order among the new 'herd'. In some collieries the horses' shoes were removed before bringing them to the surface, to prevent injuries if a fight broke out. Some horses were apparently killed during this period. After the holidays, they had to be rounded up and sent back down the pit again – it's no surprise that many miners thought that bringing the horses to the surface once a year was as cruel as leaving them underground.

Horse shows

The best-looking colliery horses would be exhibited in shows, with collieries competing with each other for the champion horse. Such 'show horses' usually led a very privileged life, often kept on light duties to preserve their appearance.

THE PD REVIEW

THE ROYAL SHOW

P.D.A.C. EXHIBIT COLLIERY HORSES

"They are very fine animals, and obviously well cared for."—H.R.H. THE DUKE OF KENT.

NOT for the first time has the idea been exploded that colliery horses are to be pitied, and that their life underground is wretched and even cruel.

In a leading article in the "Farmer and Stockbreeder," a high authority—who inspected the colliery horses at the Royal Show in Cardiff—described the display as an "eye-opener."

COLLIERY HORSES BELONGING TO P.D.A.C. EXHIBITED AT THE ROYAL SHOW, CARDIFF, JULY, 1938.
Horses and Hauliers in Charge (*read from left to right*):—"Inman," N. J. Bailey; "Captain," T. Evans; "Justice," T. Furlong; "Don," Edgar Davies; "Bedford," E. Haggett; "Andy," R. Thomas; "The Gaffer," O. Lloyd; "Penallta Emperor," W. Moseley. Standing next to "Penallta Emperor" and holding the Championship Cup is Mr. G. S. Bruce, Powell Duffryn Veterinary Surgeon.

Page Eleven

The *Powell Duffryn Review*, 1938

No. 33　　　THE P.D.　　　REVIEW　　　January, 1938

"PENALLTA EMPEROR"

ONE of the misconceptions which, for reasons unknown to us, exist in the public imagination, concerns the treatment of pit horses and ponies.

Let us, once and for all time, dispel the myth that these faithful creatures are neglected and overworked. This is not so. Horses and ponies employed at collieries either above or below ground are well-fed and well-stabled, and their hours of work are not excessive. Both colliery officials and men take the greatest pride in their charges.

We are able to reproduce a photograph of " Penallta Emperor." His record at the Shows last year is as impressive as his appearance suggests. At the Tredegar Show, he won the first prize for the best underground or cart-horse not exceeding 15.2 hands, and a cup for the best heavy horse in the Show.

At Monmouth, he gained the first prize for colliery horses, and at Abergavenny a similar award for horses working underground. In addition, he won the 2nd Prize for horses working underground at the Blackwood Show. On that occasion, he was beaten by "The Gaffer," another horse from the Powell Duffryn Associated Collieries.

" Penallta Emperor " is a brown horse, and stands 14.3 hands. We are proud of his successes, and equally so of his excellent condition which is typical of other colliery horses and ponies, and to which judges, more able than ourselves, have paid tribute.

Page Forty-Five

The show horse 'Emperor' at Penallta Colliery, illustrated in the *Powell Duffryn Review*, 1938

No. 39   THE P. D.   REVIEW   July, 1939

"OVER or THROUGH"

A COLLIERY HORSE

WRITTEN BY HIMSELF

"OVER OR THROUGH."
Ridden by Mr. H. M. Llewellyn at the Cardiff May Day Horse Show.
Photo: Western Mail.

EVERYONE laughed hilariously at the bare idea of me, a colliery horse—entering a jumping competition. Everyone, except my rider, and he only smiled, but it was the smile of confidence, not of amusement or ridicule, for he knew just what I could do. Had he not schooled me himself? Encouragement enough for any horse to do his best; and, in return, I did not mean to let him down if I could help it!

The occasion was the Cardiff May Day Horse Show, when hunters and heavy horses alike were being put through their paces, each owner with his eye on the cup that was to be given for his particular class.

Not being used to writing for magazines, I do not know the proper expression to use to describe the company in which I found myself, but of all the " swanks " and " stand-offs," commend me to the hunter class! They looked at me as though I were " mud," and, for the moment, I felt it, but a friendly pat from Cooper, for whom I've the utmost respect, as he groomed and fed me while I was at St. Fagans, brought me to my senses.

They were trying moments indeed when we all walked around the paddock, awaiting our turn to enter the ring, and I felt painfully conscious of my shape, my hairy covered heels and thick mane. For the moment, I would have given anything to have turned tail and bolted, but just as I wavered my rider climbed into the saddle, and do you know, from that moment, I felt positively inspired!

The only qualm I had was on entering the ring, when I saw all those jumps. Somehow they had grown to twice the size since I had been shown them before the class but again those gentle " hands " and a new pressure of the knees, which I had learned to understand in the last few weeks, gave me courage.

You should know that the South Walian knows a " lepper " when he sees one, and the gibes which greeted my entry were certainly perturbing. But what a sporting crowd those Welsh people are! Gibes turned to cheers when I cleared the first hurdle and only just touched the gate. Just to show them what I could do I sailed like a bird over the two poles which came next. It was my own fault when I knocked off a

Page Twenty-One

A colliery horse show jumping, illustrated in the *Powell Duffryn Review*, 1939

By F. Agar   Durham

'He's been quite impossible since the Royal Show'

> Emperor was a champion pit horse, but he didn't work underground! He was kept for going to shows.
> **Vince Court, NUM Lodge Chairman, Penallta Colliery**

Colliery horses were shown in both local horticultural and agricultural shows and national events such as the Royal Show and the International Horse Show at Olympia, which had a colliery horse section for many years. One of the strangest items at any of these shows must have been during the May Day Horse Show in Cardiff in 1939 when a Rhigos Colliery horse entered a jumping competition. Not only did he take part but he also wrote of his experiences in the Powell Duffryn Review of that year!

Not everyone was happy with the 'show horses': animal protection societies saw them as propaganda designed to mislead the public over what actually went on underground.

Left, top: A cartoon from *Coal News*, 1950s
Far left, bottom: A group of colliery horses on show in the 1930s
Left, bottom: Show horse 'Turpin' at work, Cwmgwrach Level, 1930
Above: 'Gwenny', a bay mare, in show condition with her handler, 1931

blade

Horses at Big Pit

Left: The stables at Big Pit, 2007
Above: the *Daily Sketch*, 10 April 1913

For many visitors to Big Pit: National Coal Museum, the most memorable part is the stables, still bearing the names of the horses that worked at the colliery.

By the start of the twentieth century there were around 300 horses working in coal mines in the Blaenafon area, with seventy-two in Big Pit alone.

On 7 April 1913, a fire broke out in the Mine Slope district of Big Pit. All workmen were evacuated from the workings safely and a party of officials descended the shaft to evaluate the situation. On being informed that some horses were trapped, Arthur Tucker, a manager at Blaenavon Collieries and leader of the exploring party, remarked that 'five horses was worth trying to save'.

Four men – Tucker, James Jenkins, William Bond and Frank Gratton – entered the workings, leaving instructions for others to follow if they failed to return within an hour. After twenty minutes a rescue party decided to look for them and found Gratton (the father of Graham, a former electrical engineer at Big Pit), who had been left behind to wait for them, suffering badly from exposure to poisonous gas. After several attempts, the bodies of the other three were found, lying dead in the roadway. The five horses were also killed and the fire raged for some weeks before being brought under control.

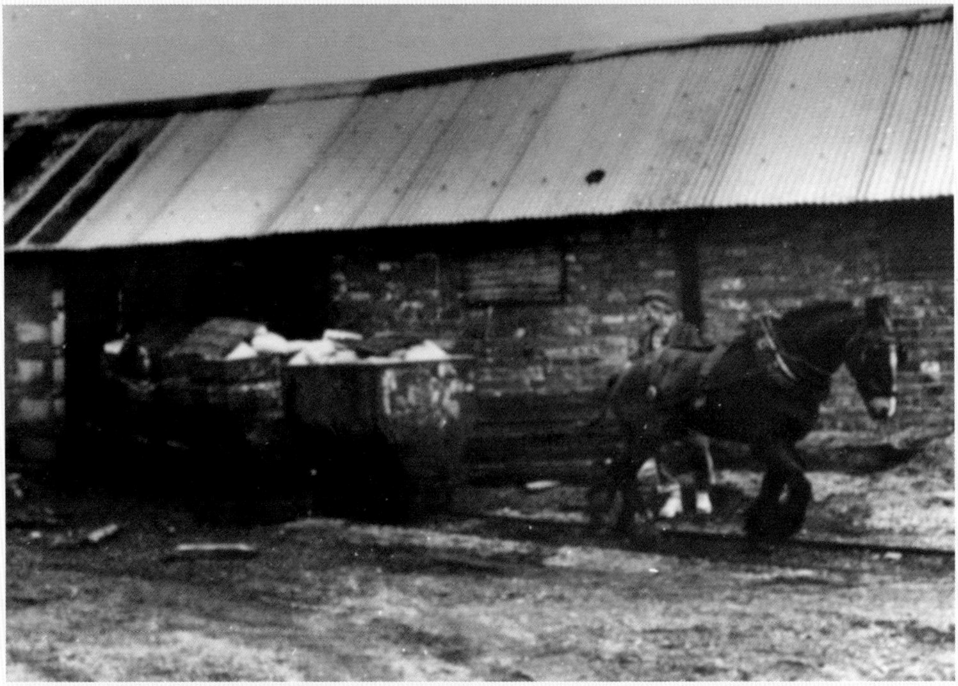

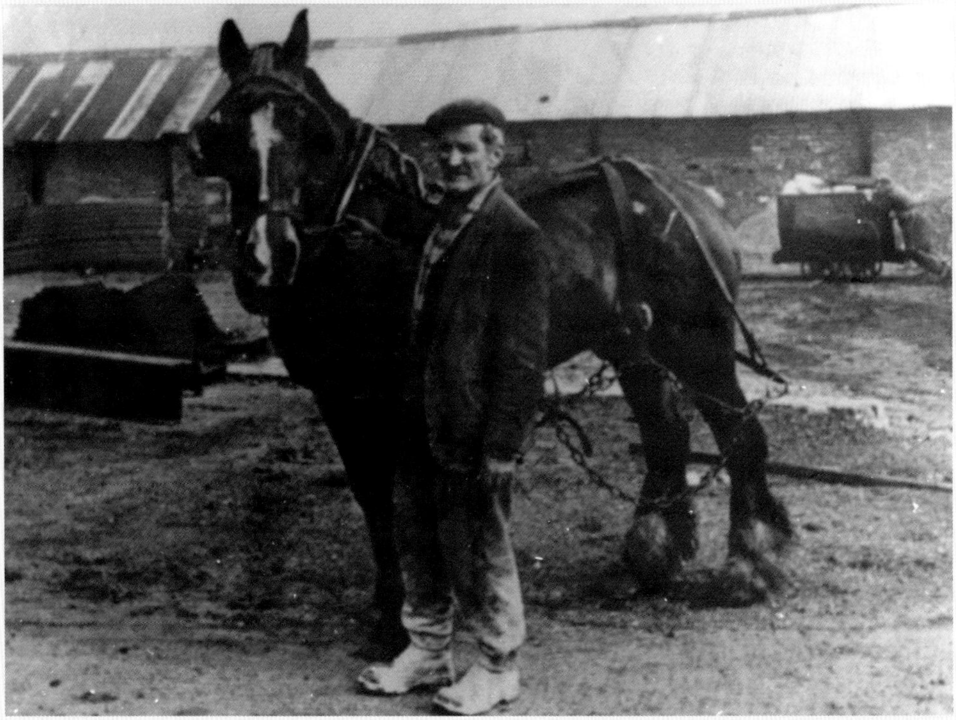

Left, top: A horse pulling drams at Big Pit, about 1970
Left, bottom: A horse on the surface at Big Pit, about 1970
Above: Big Pit's underground rocking horse, 2007

The last horse underground at Big Pit was brought up in 1972, but two were kept at work on the surface until 1974.

Aubrey Flynn was under manager at Big Pit during the 1970s and remembered the last horses at the colliery, as they were part of his responsibilities:

> They were examined by an ostler every day and well looked after. They rarely came to harm underground – in fact there were more casualties among them when they were brought to the surface for the miners' annual holidays.
>
> This was because they were washed, fed and watered twice a day when they were working. They became accustomed to the warm and dry atmosphere underground. When they came up to the surface, they sometimes caught pneumonia even though it was summer, and they would fight each other because they were so disoriented.
>
> After the last of the horses were brought up in 1972, one of the men came to me with a straight face and said that a pony had been left underground. I found this hard to believe but I felt I had to take a look. We went down to the stables and found a rocking horse in one of them. It's still there.

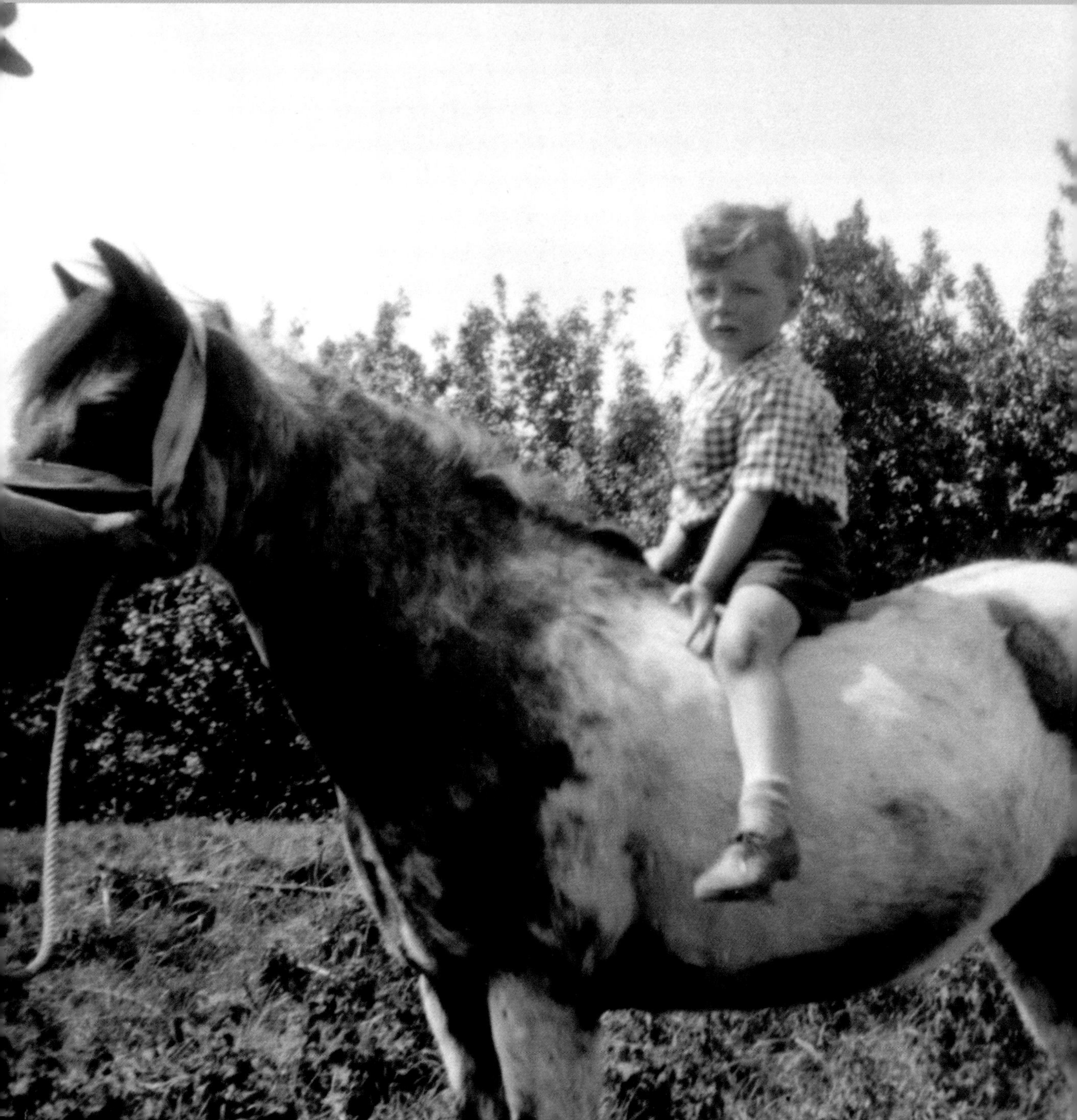

The end of the road

> In the old days ponies on the mountains were bred mainly for the coal pits, nowadays breeding must be based on the requirements of the children's riding type of pony.
> Council of the Welsh Pony and Cob Society, November 1950

In 1878 the RSPCA estimated that there were around 200,000 horses working in British mines. By 1913 the numbers had decreased to 70,000. This decline was due to the increasing mechanization of the coal mining industry. By the late nineteenth century huge underground haulage engines were moving coal in the main roadways. From the early 1900s there was a rapid increase in the use of mechanical coal conveyors and, from 1933, electric underground locomotives came into use. In 1930 the Mines Department reported that twenty-five Welsh collieries had no horses at all. However, horses remained useful, even in large modern collieries, for moving materials and equipment to and from the less accessible parts of the mine.

By the nationalization of the coal industry in 1947, there were 8,000 horses at work in Welsh mines. Twenty years later there were only 260 in National Coal Board mines and 157 in small licensed mines. By the 1980s the last National Coal Board horses were being retired but, in many licensed mines, horses were to haul coal for a few more years to come.

Left and above: Colliery horses in retirement on Anglesey, about 1960

Above: Horses on the surface at Ty Trist Colliery, on the last production day, January 1959
Right: 'Robbie' in his stable at the National Coal Mining Museum for England, 2005
Overleaf: 'Robbie' when he was still at work at Pant y Gasseg Mine, 1999

The last colliery horse?

The last working colliery horses in Britain were probably Robbie and Gremlin at Pant y Gasseg – 'horse's hollow' – a small mine near Pontypool. They were both retired in May 1999 and sent to an RSPCA rest home in Milton Keynes. However Robbie, a 15.2-hands black gelding dale horse, found retirement boring and was loaned to the National Coal Mining Museum for England in Wakefield where he joined Patch, who had formerly worked at Nant Fach Colliery in Swansea. There, he got the exercise and stimulation he needed by pulling light tubs around the site.

Gremlin had not been much used in the days before his retirement, so it is likely that Robbie has the distinction of being the last horse to have worked in a British coal mine.

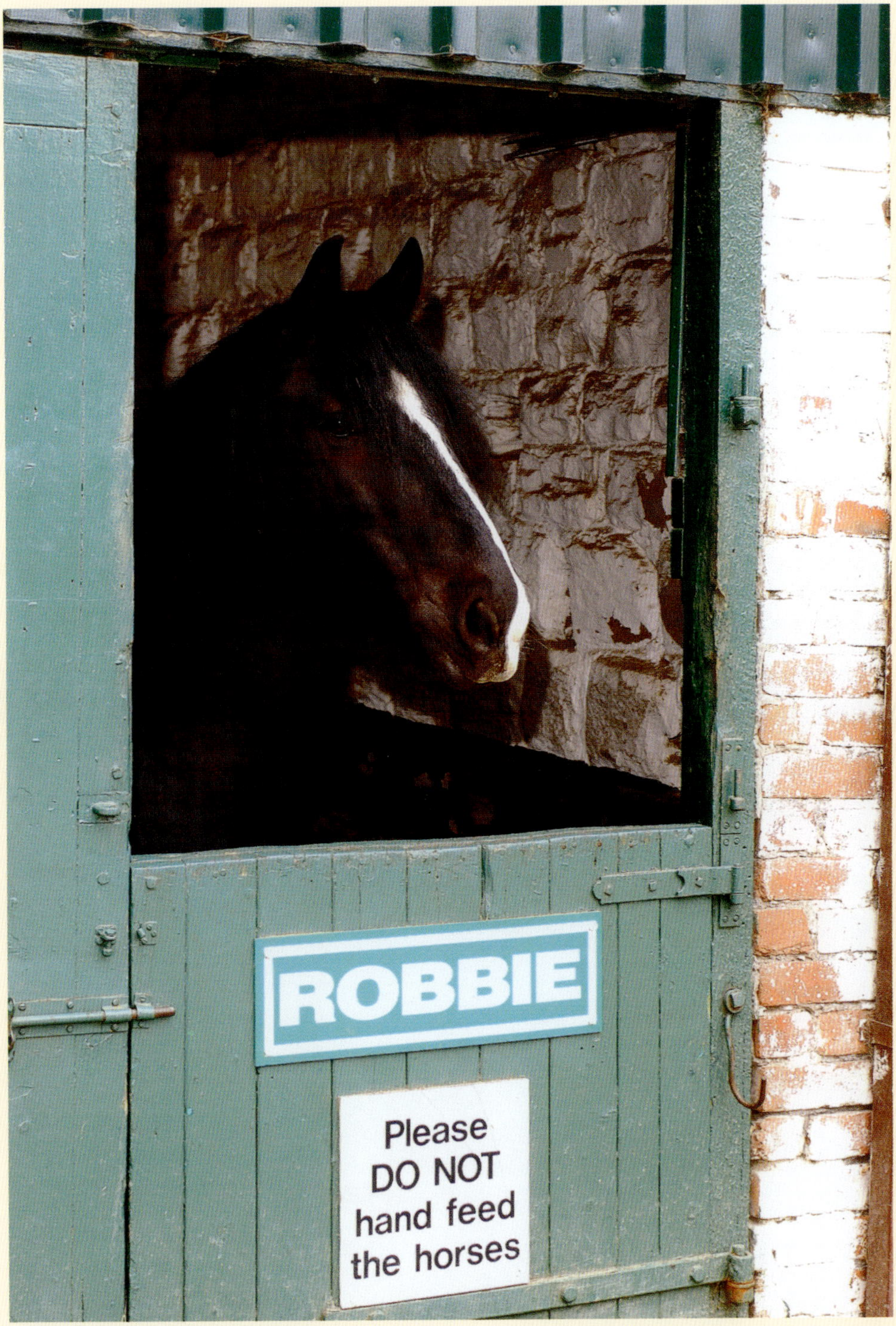
ROBBIE
Please
DO NOT
hand feed
the horses

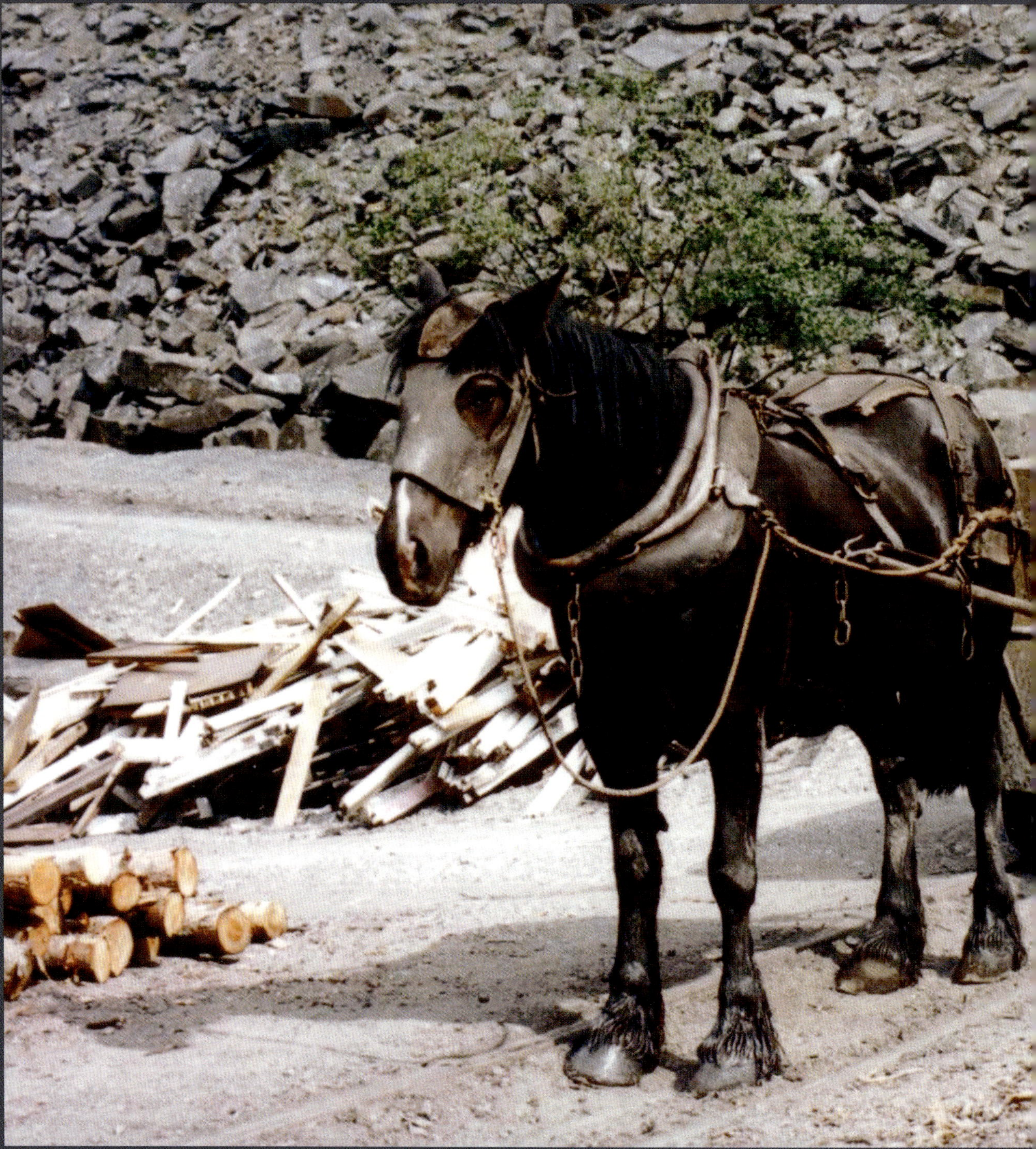

The Pit Pony's Prayer

To thee my master I offer my prayer

Feed me with food clear of dust, properly mixed with Bran and rolled oats, so that I can digest my food, also water and care for me, when the day's work is done provide me with shelter, a clean dry bed and a stall wide enough for me to lie down in comfort.

Talk to me – your voice often means as much to me as the reins. Pet me sometimes, that I may serve you the more gladly and learn to love you. Do not jerk the reins and do not whip me when going up hill. Never strike, beat or kick me when I do not understand what you mean, but give me a chance to understand you.

Watch me and if I fail to do your bidding see if something is not wrong with my harness or feet. Examine my teeth when I do not eat, I may have an ulcerated tooth and that, as you know, is very painful. Do not tie my head in an un-natural position, or take away my best defence against flies and mosquitoes by cutting off my tail.

Finally, oh my master, when my useful strength is gone do not turn me out to starve or freeze or sell me to some cruel owner to be slowly tortured or starved to death, but do thou master take my life in the kindest way and your God will reward you here and hereafter. You may not consider me irreverent if I ask this in the name of him who was born in a stable.

Amen

(Photo courtesy of Paul Jackson)

Glossary

Barhook – a drag attached to the back of a dram as a safety device, which stops it running backwards when ascending a slope.

Big pin – see shaft and gun.

Breast pad – used if a horse was 'galled' (chafed) around the neck and shoulders and couldn't pull with a collar.

Breeching – a harness strap about three inches wide, which passes behind a horse's haunches. It is used to hold the dram away from the horse while descending a slope. Also known as 'britches'.

Broken winded – an animal with a lung complaint.

Butty – name given to a fellow mine worker.

Cage – a metal platform with roof and sides in which people, animals, materials and minerals are drawn up or down a colliery shaft.

Collar – a device made from leather and fabric usually stuffed with straw which fits around the neck of a horse and is attached to the harness enabling the animal to pull loads.

Chaff – a mixture of chopped hay and oats.

Deep mine – a mine entered through a vertical shaft.

Dram – the common south Wales term for a wheeled truck used to carry coal or supplies, also known in some collieries as a tram.

Drenching frame – used to secure a horse while being treated medically.

Drenching horn – used to administer medicine to horses.

Drift mine – a mine accessed via an inclined tunnel rather than a vertical shaft.

Flean – a key used to pull the hames bars together around the collar.

Gob – part of a coal mine where coal has been removed.

Grease heel – this is caused by wet conditions and dirt. It appears on lower legs as patches of scurf; under the scurf the skin will be red and oozing.

Gun – see shaft and gun.

Hames bars – the two curved bars holding the harness to the horse's collar. Also known as an 'omz'.

Licensed Mine – on 1 January 1947 over 1,000 mines were brought into public ownership under the control of the National Coal Board. Another 450 small mines were licensed by the NCB for private operation.

Parting – a junction in an underground roadway.

Shaft and gun – a device that enabled a horse to draw a dram, also known as a 'limber' or 'limmer'. The horse was placed in the metal shaft, which was connected to a curved piece of bar known as a 'gun' by a length of metal rod known as a 'small pin'. In turn the gun was connected by a 'large pin' to the 'hitching plate' or 'draw bar', which ran the length of a dram with a connecting hole at each end.

Small pin – see shaft and gun.

Sprag – a piece of wood about eighteen inches long with pointed ends pushed into the spokes of a dram wheel to act as a brake. Specially made metal sprags were also used.

Traces – two side straps or chains that connect a harnessed horse to the load. To keep the traces apart a wooden spreader or 'swingletree' is attached to them between the horse and the load.

Tram – see dram.

Tub – the north Wales coalfield's smaller version of the south Wales dram.

Twitch – a device placed around the muzzle to restrain a horse while undergoing treatment.

A line drawing of a horse and dram, showing the 'shaft and gun' and 'harness'

Further reading

John Bright, *Pit ponies*, 1986, Batsford.
B. L. Coombes, *These poor hands*, 1939, Victor Gollancz Ltd.
Jennifer Davies, *Tales of the old horsemen*, 1997, David & Charles.
Sharon Ford and Ceri Thompson, *Big Pit: National Coal Museum*, 2005, National Museum Wales Books.
Herbert W. Hughes, *A text-book of coal-mining*, 1893, Griffin & Co.
Robert Morgan, *My lamp still burns*, 1981, Gomer Press.
Eric Squires, *Pit pony heroes*, 1974, David & Charles.
Exhibition of colliery horses, 1938, Western Mail & Echo Ltd.
Parade of underground colliery horses and pit ponies, 1931, The Monmouthshire and South Wales Coal Owner's Association.
Pit ponies, date unknown, Yorkshire Mining Museum.
Pit ponies, 1956, National Coal Board.